LEGAL RULES AND
INTERNATIONAL SOCIETY

LEGAL RULES AND INTERNATIONAL SOCIETY

Anthony Clark Arend

New York   *Oxford*   •   *Oxford University Press*   *1999*

Oxford University Press

Oxford   New York

Athens   Auckland   Bangkok   Bogotá   Buenos Aires   Calcutta
Cape Town   Chennai   Dar es Salaam   Delhi   Florence   Hong Kong   Istanbul
Karachi   Kuala Lumpur   Madrid   Melbourne   Mexico City   Mumbai
Nairobi   Paris   São Paulo   Singapore   Taipei   Tokyo   Toronto   Warsaw

and associated companies in
Berlin   Ibadan

Published by Oxford University Press, Inc.
198 Madison Avenue, New York, New York 10016

Oxford is a registered trademark of Oxford University Press

Library of Congress Cataloging-in-Publication Data
Arend, Anthony C.
Legal rules and international society / Anthony Clark Arend.
p.   cm.
Includes index.
ISBN 0-19-512710-2; 0-19-512711-0 (pbk.)
1. International law.   2. International organization.
3. International relations.   I. Title.
KZ3110.A74A35   1999
341—dc21   98-44260

1 3 5 7 9 8 6 4 2

Printed in the United States of America
on acid-free paper

For my mother,
CORA CLARK AREND,
with much love

ACKNOWLEDGMENTS

Over the course of the last several years, many individuals have contributed in one way or another to my work on this book. At Georgetown, I was encouraged by support from Eusebio Mujal-León, Robert J. Lieber, Jeff Peck, Wayne A. Davis, and Robert E. Cumby. A wide variety of individuals read portions of the manuscript. These include Thomas M. Franck, Steve Guerra, Mark Janis, Roy Godson, and James MacDougal. Clyde Wilcox, Michael Bailey, and Douglas Reed were especially helpful in providing methodological comments on chapter 3. George E. Shambaugh also provided critical assistance with chapter 4. Alexander Wendt similarly provided invaluable assistance with chapter 4 and has been a consistent source of encouragement for this project. Thomas Banchoff provided much help regarding my discussion of the European Union in chapter 4. Throughout this process, George E. Little has been of invaluable assistance as my teaching assistant and friend. I have also appreciated the assistance of April L. Morgan, Jason Davidson, Bridget Grimes, Mira Sucharov, Kerry Pace, and David Boyer.

Three of my colleagues and very good friends—Christopher C. Joyner, Charles E. Pirtle, and Christopher M. Rossomondo—read the entire manuscript. I am especially indebted to their assistance. Chris Joyner's knowledge of international law and his critical eye were of great help. He has been a constant source of support and encouragement throughout my academic career. Chris Rossomondo's legal skills and his understanding of international politics also helped refine the manuscript. Charlie Pirtle's willingness to share his books, time, and insight proved to be an important motivation. Not only did he read the entire work once, but he also gave multiple readings to several chapters. He also suggested a number of the examples that I employ to illustrate the theory.

Elizabeth A. Campbell has been an inspiration to my work over the years. Phillip A. Karber has also been an important source of support—especially with my work on Constructivism. Daniel R. Porterfield has provided encouragement in light of a variety of other activities that have occupied my time.

I am also indebted to Robert J. Beck. Bob and I have worked on several collaborative projects over the last ten years. It was really Bob that introduced me to many aspects of international relations theory and the importance of international relations theory for understanding international law. I owe a great debt to him for the hundreds of conversations and his suggestions for this project.

I would also be remise if I did not acknowledge several other individuals who have influenced my thinking on these issues. William V. O'Brien was my undergraduate mentor. He taught me international law nearly twenty years ago and has been a source of support over the years. It is often amazing that when I reread what I have written, I can frequently see Bill's influence. Inis L. Claude was my mentor in graduate school. Inis's dedication to scholarship and his way of thinking about international relations have also had a tremendous influence upon me. John Norton Moore was my "law mentor" while I was in graduate school. John introduced me to the New Haven approach and supported my international legal scholarship. Adam Watson was also a professor of mine in graduate school. He introduced me to Hedley Bull and the English School. This approach to international relations also had an important impact on my thinking.

I also wish to thank Thomas LeBien and MaryBeth Branigan from Oxford University Press for all their assistance and skill.

Finally, I wish to thank my mother—Cora Clark Arend. I have dedicated this work to her. It is impossible to do justice in a few words to describe the support, encouragement, and prayers that she has provided to me throughout my life. She clearly is the one person without whom this work would not have been possible.

CONTENTS

LEGAL RULES AND INTERNATIONAL SOCIETY

INTRODUCTION

As the world enters the twenty-first century, one of the greatest uncertainties facing both scholars and practitioners of international relations is the future of the international system. As the cold war was coming to an end, many commentators began to speak of the emergence of a "New World Order." While it was unclear precisely what that phrase meant—indeed, it undoubtedly meant many different things to different people—the concept of the New World Order expressed a hope that the international system was becoming more peaceful and just.[1] In such a new system, many assumed international legal rules would be strengthened and multilateral organizations would play a significant role in managing international conflict. But as the tragedies of Somalia, Rwanda, and the Balkans played themselves out, the expectations for a better international system seemed premature. International legal rules seemed impotent and international organizations seemed incapable. Many believed that the world would settle back into a competitive balance-of-power system.

Nonetheless, in the midst of these tumultuous world events an increasing amount of scholarship is being devoted to the study of norms and institutions. As this study proceeds, one element that deserves a fresh look is international law. The purpose of this book is to attempt to provide such an examination of international law. I believe the time is especially propitious for this examination for several reasons. First, there is a need to rehabilitate the status of international law within the political science community. Second, there is a need to provide a methodology of international law that returns the discipline to an examination of empirical data. Third, the changing nature of the international system requires that certain fundamental principles of international law be reexamined. Let me say a few words about each of these points.

INTERNATIONAL LAW AND POLITICAL SCIENCE

In a 1990 essay on recent works on international legal rules, law professor Phillip Trimble observed that "[t]o academics and practitioners alike, international law is a peripheral enterprise."[2] He then went on to cite a report prepared by John King Gamble and Natalie S. Shields in which they argue that "many academics still regard international law as . . . a 'fringe' specialty, well meaning, even noble, but naive and largely irrelevant to the real world."[3] Within the discipline of political science, this skepticism toward international law has been especially high. During most of the post-World War II era, realism (both classical realism and its successor, structural realism) has been the dominate paradigm for understanding international relations. For the vast majority of structural realists, international rules—whether actually called "international law," seen as an element of an "international regime," or termed "international norms"—are largely epiphenomenal. The rules may exist, but they do not exert an independent influence on state behavior. Accordingly, the study of international rules is not an extremely useful pursuit for political scientists. They would make better use of their time by studying the political and economic factors that really affect behavior.

Notwithstanding these rather pessimistic views, however, scholarly interest in international rules has been increasing over the past several years. Confronted with the difficulty of explaining cooperation among international actors under the logic of the realist paradigm, another approach to international relations has emerged in recent years—institutionalism. In contrast to the realists, institutionalists assert that international rules and institutions can indeed play a significant role in international relations and that a proper understanding of the international system requires an understanding of these rules and institutions.

Interestingly enough, however, much of the institutionalist literature does not explicitly discuss *international law*. Instead, the institutionalist writings examine more general concepts such as "principles," "norms," and "rules," ignoring the distinctiveness of international legal rules and the international legal system.[4] Why has this been the case? One reason may be the legacy of the realists. After years of blasting international law and international legal scholars as irrelevant to international relations, the realists may have seemingly turned the words "international law" into a red herring. As a consequence, while the institutionalists may have wished to reintroduce normative concerns to international relations, they may have been fearful of doing so with a discussion of "international law." The safer, social science-sounding words like "norms" and "institutions" may have seemed more appropriate. Another reason may have been the lack of familiarity with the substance of international law. It is quite difficult to discuss the role legal rules play in international relations without a reasonable understanding of what those rules are and how they are constituted. And yet perhaps another reason may be that even the institutionalists may view international law as formal rules that do indeed bear little resemblance to the realities of international relations. They may think of international law not as a dynamic set of rules that are created and changed through state practice, but rather as stultified, dust-covered treaties that have no connection to the real world—the Kellogg-Briand Pact, for example.

'why is law necessary?'

A basic proposition of this book is that understanding international law—international *legal* rules—is essential to the study of international relations. As Professor Andrew Hurrell asserts, "it is international law that provides the essential bridge between the procedural rules of the game and the structural principles that specify how the game of power and interests is defined and how the identity of the players is established."[5] International law, he continues, "provides a framework for understanding the processes by which rules and norms are constituted and a sense of obligation engendered in the minds of policy-makers."[6] In short, understanding the nature of international *legal* rules is crucial to an understanding of international relations generally. They are different in nature from other types of rules and play a distinctive role in international politics.

Fortunately, some political scientists are beginning to recognize the distinctiveness of legal rules.[7] Under the leadership of scholars such as Lea Brilmayer, Harold Koh, Anne-Marie Slaughter, Kenneth Abbott, John King Gamble, Oran Young, Christopher C. Joyner, Friedrich Kratochwil, Charlotte Ku, as well as Professor Hurrell, there has been a growing dialogue between international legal scholars and political scientists.[8] Indeed, in recent years a number of workshops and conferences have been organized specifically to further this dialogue. These include events sponsored by the Academic Council on the United Nations System, the Schell Center for Human Rights at Yale Law School, and the American Society of International Law. This book seeks to encourage this dialogue and help reverse the practice of neglect that international law suffered at the hands of many political scientists in the past. Needless to say, some of the discussion of international relations theory will be quite familiar to international relations scholars, and some of the examination of international law will not seem new to international legal scholars. But to be truly interdisciplinary, I believe it is necessary to provide sufficient background so that scholars from both fields can appreciate the other arguments that this book seeks to advance.[9]

INTERNATIONAL LAW
AND EMPIRICAL DATA

But even while the political scientists were all but ignoring international legal rules, much scholarship was flourishing within the discipline of international law. Throughout the cold war, legal scholars were authoring a plethora of treatises, casebooks, and articles. Indeed, with changes in the international system and developments in technology, scholars had more substantive legal issues with which to grapple—outer space, the deep sea-bed, self-determination, human rights, and others. But unfortunately, a great deal of this scholarship has been doctrinal in nature.[10] By that I mean that scholarly debates about what a particular rule of law is tend to center around different conceptions raised by different scholars. For example, when examining the question of whether there is a rule of international law permitting the use of force for humanitarian intervention, the discussion may focus on the value of, let us say, Professor Michael Reisman's approach versus Professor Fernando Tesón's approach. As a consequence, the debate frequently centers on the scholars' paradigms and not the behavior of the international actors that they are supposed to be evaluating.

In theory, legal scholars do not create rules of international law; rather they muster empirical evidence that supports the existence of a particular rule. But to do this, they need to examine real-world behavior. Increasingly, legal scholarship seems to have been removed from this basic, but often very time consuming and complicated, exploration of the behavior of international actors.[11] This may be attributable to several factors.

First, in the old days of international law, there was only one international actor—the state. And there were not that many states in the international system. Hence, to do a thorough examination of customary state practice in 1920, did not require an examination of all that many states. At present, however, there are 191[12] states in the international system, and there are a variety of other international actors whose behavior may affect the development of international law.

Second, it is difficult to evaluate empirical data once it has been collected. Perhaps a scholar can obtain evidence of state behavior, but how is he or she to determine whether there is sufficient state practice for a putative rule to constitute international law? It is one thing to note, as does Article 38 of the Statute of the International Court of Justice, that a rule of customary international law requires there to be "a general practice accepted as law."[13] But how much practice is required for there to be a "general practice?" Do all 191 states have to participate in this practice? Indeed, what is a practice? And how does an investigator determine if the practice is "accepted as law?" Is mere rhetorical endorsement sufficient? Or is more required? In short, it is difficult to develop a common methodology for analyzing and evaluating practice.

A second basic proposition of this book is that the determination of rules of international law must be rooted in empirical analysis. Accordingly, it will seek to provide a useful methodology that will enable scholars and practitioners to examine the practice of international actors and evaluate that practice.

THE CHANGING NATURE OF
THE INTERNATIONAL SYSTEM

It is almost axiomatic to say that the international system is in a state of flux. With the end of the cold war and the seeming rise of multilateral institutions, two fundamental aspects of the international system may be undergoing change: the structure and the actors.[14]

First, it is quite clear that the bipolar system that dominated the globe for over forty years no longer reflects reality. Instead, the structure is in transition. Some suggest that the structure is moving toward a multipolar system, while others contend that it is a unipolar system.

Second, there has also been an increase in the role played by a host of nonstate actors. At the broadest level, international governmental organizations from the United Nations to the European Union to NATO to the Organization of American States have been much more involved in international relations since the end of the cold war. Similarly, nongovernmental organizations like the International Committee on the Red Cross, Amnesty International, and Greenpeace have also been more active than in past years. In addition, other nonstate entities such as the Bosnian Serbs, the Palestinians, and the Kurds have been engaged in international negotiations and concluding international agreements in an unprecedented fashion.

A third proposition of this book is that the changing structure of the international system and the new role of nonstate actors *may* affect the nature of international law. In particular, these developments may have an important impact on the way in which international law is made.

As noted earlier, under traditional international legal theory, international law was created by states. If nonstate actors are entering into the international negotiating process in different ways, scholars may need to reassess their assumptions about how international law is constituted. Moreover, if the structure of the international system is changing, the role that legal rules play in international relations may also be changing.

In light of these three propositions, this book seeks to accomplish four main goals. First, it will attempt to demonstrate the importance of recognizing the distinctiveness of international *legal* rules. To do this, it will differentiate legal rules from other types of rules that exist in the international arena—moral rules, rules of the game, rules of etiquette, and so on—and will show that legal rules are qualitatively different from other rules. Second, this work will propose a methodology for determining the existence of a rule of international law. This methodology, it is hoped, will serve both scholars and practitioners as they evaluate state practice. Third, it will seek to demonstrate the relevance of international legal rules to the interactions of international actors in the contemporary world. To this end, this book will examine several competing theories of international relations and explore the implications of these theories for the role of legal rules in international society. Drawing upon constructivist theory, this book will reach several conclusions about the critical role legal rules do play in international politics in the contemporary international system. Fourth, this work will examine certain changes that may be occurring in this system and explore the implications of these possible changes for international legal rules.

In order to accomplish these tasks, this book is divided into six chapters. Chapter 1 will examine the variety of rules that exist at the international level. Chapter 2 will discuss the creation of international legal rules. Chapter 3 will set forth my methodology for determining the existence of a rule of international law. Chapter 4 will look at the relevance of international legal rules to international relations. Chapter 5 will examine possible scenarios for the evolution of international law. Finally, chapter 6 will provide the conclusion for this work.

NOTES

1. See Anthony Clark Arend, The United Nations and the New World Order, 81 *Georgetown L. J.* (1993) for an examination of a variety of meanings of the phrase "New World Order."

2. Phillip R. Trimble, International Law, World Order, and Critical Legal Studies, 42 *Stan. L. Rev.* 811 (1990).

3. John King Gamble, Jr. & Natalie S. Shields, International Legal Scholarship: A Perspective on Teaching and Publishing, 39 *J. Legal Educ.* 39, 40 (1989).

4. Hurrell explains that "the quest for rigour (and perhaps an excessive desire to avoid the sins of idealism) has led to far too wholesale a dismissal of the need to understand both the specific character and the technical features of the international legal system." Andrew Hurrell, International Society and the Study of Regimes: A Reflective Approach, in Volker Rittberger, ed., *Regime Theory and International Relations* 49, 72 (1993).

5. Id. at 72.

6. Id.

7. As Professor Slaughter has written:

International law and international politics cohabit the same conceptual space. Together they comprise the rules and the reality of "the international system," an intellectual construct that lawyers, political scientists, and policymakers use to describe the world they study and seek to manipulate. As a distinguished group of international lawyers and a growing number of political scientists have recognized, it makes little sense to study one without the other.

Anne-Marie Slaughter, International Law in a World of Liberal States, 6 *European J. Int'l L.* 503 (1995). One example of a recent work that seeks to explore differing research methods used in international law and international relations is Charlotte Ku & Thomas G. Weiss, eds., *Toward Understanding Global Governance: The International Law and International Relations Toolbox* (1998).

8. A most recent—and outstanding—discussion of the nature of interdisciplinary scholarship in this area is Anne-Marie Slaughter, Andrew S. Tulumello & Stepan Wood, International Law and International Relations Theory: A New Generation of Interdisciplinary Scholarship, 92 *Am. J. Int'l L.* 367 (1998). These three scholars examine both how international legal scholars are making use of international relations theory and how international relations scholars are using international law. They also "explore how IR and IL scholars might collaborate most profitably in the future," id. at 383, by

suggesting a "Collaborative Research Agenda." Id. at 385. In addition, an excellent bibliography of interdisciplinary works is included.

9. Indeed, this is an observation made by one of the anynomous reviewers of an earlier draft of this manuscript.

10. See Anthony Carty, *The Decay of International Law* 13 (1986) ("At present doctrine is understood to afford evidence of the existence of rules of international law.").

11. This is a point that has been made by Professor William V. O'Brien.

12. This figure includes three "freely associated states": The Federated States of Micronesia, the Republic of the Marshall Islands, and Palau. It also includes Serbia-Montenegro as one state. I owe this information to Professor Charles E. Pirtle.

13. Statute of the International Court of Justice, art. 38, para. 1 (1945).

14. I am indebted to Professor Charles E. Pirtle for emphasizing these two factors.

ONE

THE VARIETY OF INTERNATIONAL RULES

As noted earlier, the political science community recently has witnessed a new flourishing of normative discussions. Scholars from both the institutionalist and realist camps have engaged in lively debates about the role of norms and institutions. The pages of such journals as *International Organization, Political Science Quarterly*, and even *International Security* are filled with extensive examinations of both sides of the debate. Initially, regime theory helped reinvigorate normative discourse into the mainstream of international relations theory.[1] As scholars asked if "regimes matter," they were, in effect, asking the crucial question: Do normative concerns matter in contemporary international relations? Most recently, constructivists have been raising important questions about the role of norms in international politics.[2]

As these discussions proceed, it is critical that distinctions be drawn among the different kinds of rules that exist at the international level. In order to appreciate the distinctiveness of international legal rules in particular, it is necessary to differentiate legal rules from other types of rules. Even though some commentators may equate the term "rules" automatically with "law," all rules that operate in international interactions are not legal in nature. Rather there are a variety of rules that

heavy discussion of norms

major question

dist. btwn legal rlgs + other rules

—not all rules = legal

3

have different characteristics. The legal requirement for coastal states to grant innocent passage through the territorial sea, for example, is fundamentally different in nature from the rule of protocol regarding the welcoming of a visiting head of state.

Although it is impossible to provide an exhaustive examination of each and every type of rule, this chapter seeks to provide a basic description of several types that may play roles in international politics and then to define international law. First, it will set the stage for a discussion of rules by very briefly exploring different "normative categories" that figure in the literature. Second, it will attempt to differentiate moral rules, legal rules, and several other types of rules. Finally, drawing upon this understanding of legal rules generally, it will examine the nature of international law—that is, of *international* legal rules.

NORMATIVE CATEGORIES

In normative discussions, scholars often use different words to describe what might be called different "normative categories." Professor Stephen Krasner's definition of a "regime" provides an example of this lexical undertaking. In his oft-cited 1982 article, he describes regimes as "sets of implicit or explicit principles, norms, rules, and decision-making procedures around which actors' expectations converge in a given area of international relations."[3] Without at this point getting into a discussion of the regime concept per se, it is useful to note that Krasner is differentiating four normative categories: principles, norms, rules, and decision-making procedures. He goes on to define these four concepts. "Principles," according to him, "are beliefs of fact, causation, and rectitude."[4] In other words, principles form a normative category that is at the highest level of abstraction. They constitute the fundamental assumptions that underlie a particular regime and define its very nature. "Norms," says Krasner, "are standards of behavior defined in terms of rights and obligations."[5] Norms thus would be more specific than principles. In essence, they would be elaborations upon rights and obligations that would flow from the broader principles. Still more specific are "rules." According to Krasner, they form "specific prescriptions or proscriptions for action."[6] Rules would thus seem to provide detailed guidance for behavior at what might be called the "operational" level. Finally, "decision-making procedures are prevailing practices for making and implementing collective choice."[7] These procedures are thus not necessarily more specific than rules, but simply operate in a different context.

While Krasner's distinctions may be useful, his typology is problematic since it could be interpreted as claiming that these are discrete categories upon which there can be agreement. But, in fact, whether something is a "principle" or a "norm" or a "rule" could be quite debatable. Is, for example, the inviolability of a diplomat a "principle," a "norm" or a "rule?" It could be argued that since it sets forth a basic belief of rectitude—that is, it is legally wrong to arrest a diplomat—it would constitute a principle. Yet, it could be contended that it is a norm since, it defines the right of a sending state not to have its diplomats interfered with and the concomitant obligation of a receiving state not to interfere with the diplomats of the sending state. Finally, it could be argued that diplomatic inviolability is a rule, since it establishes a specific proscription.[8]

Without ultimately passing judgment on this or other categorizations, I will use the word "rule" in this book as an inclusive term to describe all types of normative categories.[9] I recognize that there are differences in levels of generalization among rules. For example, it is clear that the right of "freedom of navigation" is nowhere near as specific a normative rule as the right "to draw straight base lines" under certain circumstances. Similarly, the rules concerning the procedure for voting in the United Nations Security Council are different in nature from rules relating to human rights. Nonetheless, the generic term "rules" is sufficiently general to encompass all these examples.

But if the word rule will be used to describe the whole range of normative categories, what kinds of rules exist? What are the distinctions among the rules that may exist at the international level?

TYPES OF RULES

Moral Rules

Perhaps the most ancient kind of rule associated with human interaction is moral rules. Virtually, all the world's great religions have codified sets of rules that define right and wrong behavior. The Ten Com-
mandments, the Code of Hammarabi, and other ancient texts set out
fundamental moral rules. Even nonreligious philosophical frameworks
make certain assertions about moral behavior. But how can a *moral* rule
be defined?

Simply put, a moral rule is one that obliges the actor to behave in
a particular way. As H. L. A. Hart notes, "moral rules impose obligations and withdraw certain areas of conduct from the free option of
the individuals to do as" he or she chooses.[10] A moral rule says that a
person *must* do something or, conversely, *must not* do something. But
the same could be said for legal rules. In the United States, for example, an obligation is imposed upon an individual to drive on the
right side of the road. He or she is not "free" to drive on the left. What
then makes moral rules distinctive?

One of the great philosophical debates surrounds the nature of
morality. In particular, there is much disagreement about the origins
of moral rules. Many thinkers—from Plato to Augustine to Ghandi—
would claim that moral rules have their source in the metaphysical.
Morality, they would assert, comes from God or from a vision of the
Good or some other transempirical source. Other commentators would
argue that moral rules can be discovered through careful observation
of empirical reality. By examining our environment, they might argue,
certain rules necessary for human survival can be determined.[11] Still
others would contend that moral rules are merely conventional. They
are rules of behavior that have been agreed upon, either explicitly or
implicitly, by the members of a particular society. It clearly lies beyond the scope of this work to enter into an extensive philosophical
discussion of the origins of morality. For our purposes, it is sufficient
to note several characteristics of moral rules that serve to distinguish
them from other rules, especially legal rules.

First, irrespective of whether the source of a moral rule is found in the metaphysical, the physical, or the conventional, there seems to be broad agreement that moral rules are not the product of a political process. In other words, it is not the state or some other political authority that creates moral rules. Political authorities may follow moral rules; they may even enact preexisting moral rules as laws. But the rules of morality do not have their ultimate origin in these authorities. The source may be God; it may be "society"; it may be "human nature." But it is not the state.

Second, just as moral rules are not created through the political process, they are also not enforceable—as moral rules—by political authorities. Clearly, if a moral rule has been enacted into a legal rule, then that *legal* rule is enforceable by political authorities. But a moral rule *qua* moral rule is not so enforceable. So, for example, there would seem to be universal agreement that it is a moral rule that persons are not to commit murder.[12] That moral rule has also been made a legal rule by political authorities in all states in the international system. Consequently, if an individual commits murder, the political authorities in a state may take action against the individual for violating the *legal* rule. There are, however, numerous moral rules that have not been made legal rules and are thus not enforceable by political authorities. Many societies consider it to be morally wrong to lie. Yet, in these same societies, only certain types of lying have been legally proscribed— perjury, libel, slander, etc. If I tell a lie in court while under oath, I can be punished by the state for perjury. If, however, I promise to take a friend to the airport and do not show up, the state cannot impose a sanction upon me.

It is, of course, possible that there may be some form of sanction for violating moral rules outside the realm of the political. Many religions allow religious leaders or institutions to impose certain punishments on a coreligionist if that person fails to observe rules of morality. Certain Christian churches, for example, may excommunicate a person who commits blasphemy or engages in certain types of behavior. Moreover, many religions assert that individuals who violate moral rules will be punished by other than earthly powers. This punishment may take the form of divine punishment in this life or in the life beyond. But with the exception of theocracies where the moral rules have also been made legal rules, it is not the political authorities who enforce morality.

Finally, moral rules are different from other types of rules because of the nature of the obligation engendered by moral rules. As noted earlier, moral rules are not created by the political process and are not enforceable through the political process. Thus, for rules of morality there is a sense in which the obligation to follow the rules is owed to something beyond the political. I perceive myself constrained to follow a moral rule not because of my relationship to the body politic, but because of my relationship to some "higher" normative order. I may owe the obligation to God, to "society," or to my "inner self," but I do not owe it to something political.

Are there universal moral rules at the international level? Many a discussion has centered around this question. Given the diverse philosophical and religious frameworks out of which the peoples of the world operate, some observers would argue that there can be no truly *universal* moral rules. Perhaps there could be moral rules that exist within certain different cultural groupings—"the West," "the Islamic World," and so on.[13] But, as the argument goes, there can be no moral rules that encompass the entire international community. The world is simply too diverse. Other scholars would contend that there are at least *some* moral rules that are universal. Professor Fernando Tesón, for example, argues that there are certain fundamental principles of justice that transcend political boundaries.[14]

It lies beyond the scope of this work to plumb the depths of this important philosophical question. It is, however, not necessary that there be a complete set of common moral rules in order for there to be universal *legal* rules. Given the divergent nature of the two kinds of rules, the existence of one is not contingent upon the existence of the other.

Legal Rules

In light of this brief discussion of moral rules, the next type of rule to distinguish is legal rules. How can a legal rule be defined? Just as different definitions of morality abound, so too do different definitions of law or legal rules. In fact, each of the great jurisprudential schools has formulated various versions of the meaning of the word "law." —Several meanings of Law

One of the earliest approaches to jurisprudence is the natural law school. Beginning with Stoic thought and continuing through Christian medieval thinking, natural law dominated the philosophy of law for centuries. Even today, there is a great deal of natural law thinking reflected in scholarship. Discussions relating to human rights and "just" uses of force, for example, often draw heavily upon the natural law tradition.[15] Even some elements of feminist scholarship share certain natural law propositions.[16] For natural law writers, there exist certain fundamental principles of right and wrong behavior that can be known by all rational creatures. In *De Res Publica*, Cicero explained that there was "a true law—namely, right reason—which is in accordance with nature, applies to all" persons "and is unchangeable and eternal."[17] For the Christian natural law thinker Thomas Aquinas, all law could be understood in terms of four categories: eternal law, divine law, natural law, and human law.[18] Eternal law, for Aquinas, represented the ultimate law of the universe. This type of law was fully known only by God. Divine law was then the portion of the eternal law that God made known to human beings through revelation. Natural law was the "participation of the eternal law in the rational creature."[19] In other words, natural law was the portion of the eternal law that human beings could know through reason. Finally, human law was what we would term "positive" law. It was law created by various political authorities. Significantly, however, Aquinas believed that human law was not really "law" unless it conformed with the natural law. A king or parliament might duly enact a rule, but if it violated the tenets of the natural law, it could not be properly considered "law." Following upon this logic, for natural law theorists, legal rules would be those rules derived from and consistent with these fundamental moral principles.

While this approach has had a profound effect on thinking about both morality and law, I believe it raises some difficulties in the contemporary world. While moral rules may serve to provide the basis for formulating legal rules and while many legal rules reflect the substance of moral rules, legal rules are not automatically deducible from moral rules. As Hart argues, "theories that make this close assimilation of law to morality seem, in the end, often to confuse one kind of obligatory conduct with another, and leave insufficient room for differences in kind between legal and moral rules and for divergences in their requirements."[20] As noted above, moral rules—which may indeed play a critical role in behavior—give rise to a different kind of obligation. They create an obligation that is owed to something beyond the body politic. With legal rules, there is a perception that the obligation to abide by the rules is precisely an obligation owed to the body politic.

Moreover, if law and morality are conflated it becomes nearly impossible to evaluate the moral sufficiency of a particular law. In particular, such conflation could lead to one of two fatal errors. On the one hand, an observer could assume that if a particular behavior had been made legal, that such behavior was therefore moral. Thus, a German citizen living during the time of National Socialism could conclude that Nazi laws regarding the treatment of Jews and other minorities were moral merely because they were law—that which is legal must be moral. Or, on the other hand, one could take a Thomistic approach and conclude that a law that did not comply with certain moral rules was simply "not really the law." That approach, however, would also inhibit efforts to change immoral laws. During the civil rights movement in the United States, for example, it would have been useless to say that segregation laws were not "really law" and to go about business as usual. Instead, these laws were acknowledged as existing laws, but were criticized as *immoral* laws and thus in need of change. In short, by viewing law and morality as different kinds of obligations, it is possible to provide a moral evaluation of a particular law, and, conversely, to provide a legal evaluation of a moral rule.

Legal positivists take another approach to the nature of law. While there are many different versions of positivism, positivists typically assert that law is a set of rules that are created by political authorities. The laws are thus "posited" by some human authority. Accordingly, law becomes the product of the political process and enforceable through the political process. Legal obligation is owed to the body politic. This understanding does, I believe, capture the essence of law and thus the distinctiveness of legal rules.

Some positivists, however, claim that sanction is necessary for a rule to constitute a legal rule. John Austin, for example, considers law to be the command of a superior to an inferior, where the superior has the capability of imposing a sanction upon the inferior for noncompliance.[21] This Austinian view of law has had a profound effect on much subsequent legal thought. There are, however, a number of practical problems with this approach. Setting aside for a moment the problem sanction poses for international law, even much domestic law does not stand up to the sanction requirement. The oft-cited example is the famous *Steel Seizure* case.[22] When President Truman ordered the seizure of the steel mills during the Korean War, the U.S. Supreme Court ruled his action unconstitutional. The Court, however, had no means of enforcing the decision. The president, after all, is the individual charged by the Constitution with executing the law. Nonetheless, the Court's decision was deemed to be legally binding on the president despite the inability of the Court to force Truman to comply. Moreover, at a deeper level, no domestic law can fundamentally be dependent upon a sanction. Even though there are generally sanctions to punish those that violate the law, the efficacy of domestic law cannot ultimately depend upon those sanctions. Instead, the law is contingent upon perceptions of legitimacy.[23] If even a very small percentage of the population of the United States—2 percent for example—believed that a particular law was illegitimate and refused to obey it, no amount of coercive power present in the state could enforce compliance. It is thus the perception of legitimacy that makes the rule law and not the guarantee of sanction. It is enough that actors regard the rules as binding and, accordingly, believe that a sanction would be appropriate for a violation of such rules.

This example thus introduces another element of law that needs to be clarified. It is indeed possible for other kinds of rules to be produced through the political processes—rules of the game, for instance. One of the distinctive characteristics of law, however, is that the parties that create it and those to whom it is addressed, regard it as "law." This may sound tautological: a rule is a legal rule because it is regarded as a legal rule. But it is an extremely important characteristic. Actors perceive law to be of a different normative character than moral rules or rules of the game. They regard it as *legally* binding.[24]

Drawing upon the insights of positivism, I believe that the nature of legal rules can be summarized as follows. First, legal rules are binding. That is, they are obligatory. The actor to whom they are addressed has an obligation to carry out the rule. Second, legal rules are produced through a political process. This process could take many forms. It could be extremely institutionalized. There could be a centralized legislative body—a congress or a parliament—that produces written laws. Or the process could be decentralized—like the process whereby common law is produced in the Anglo-American tradition. Third, legal rules are enforceable through a political process. Even though there is no requirement that there be a guaranteed sanction, it is accepted by the actors that enforcement of the legal rules through the political process would be legitimate. Fourth, the obligation to carry out the legal rule is an obligation owed to the body politic—the city, the county, the province, the country, or even the international system. Fifth, both those actors who create the rules and those to whom the rules are addressed regard the rules as "legal" rules.

Other Rules

In addition to moral rules and legal rules, there are also a host of other kinds of rules that function in social systems. While numerous typologies could be developed, I will examine three other types of rules: rules of etiquette, rules of the game, and descriptive rules. Without engaging in a lengthy examination of these kinds of rules, several comments can be offered.

Rules of etiquette are rules of social behavior that are neither legally nor morally required. Yet, there is some sense of obligation to perform these rules. For example, it is neither immoral nor illegal to eat one's food underneath the table. Nonetheless, rules of politeness would oblige a person not to take such action. Similarly, at the international level there are rules of protocol that are not legally obligatory, but if violated, would be regarded as an insult by certain parties. There may, for example, be a rule of international protocol that the visiting head of state must be given a twenty-one-gun salute upon entering the territory of the state. While this rule may generally be followed out of a sense of obligation, it is not regarded as a rule of law or a rule of morality; it is not seen as legally or morally obligatory. As a consequence, a legal sanction would not be considered to be an appropriate response to a violation of such a rule. This, of course, does not mean that grave political consequences could not result from the breaching of a rule of etiquette, but simply that legal sanction would not be considered appropriate. Bolivia might file protests if Egypt only fired a nineteen-gun-salute, but Bolivia would not even contemplate taking Egypt to the International Court of Justice for such breach of protocol.

Yet another type of rule might be called "rules of the game." This expression has been used by numerous international relations theorists to describe a variety of different things. For Professor Raymond Cohen, the phrase "rules of the game" is the broad, inclusive term that encompasses all varieties of rules. He contends that rules of the game "are taken to include general norms of behaviour, aspects of international law, and rules which are created by formal and informal understanding, or are contained in the 'spirit' of agreements, verbal 'gentlemen's' agreements and different kinds of tacit understanding."[25] Given this book's fundamental thesis that legal rules are distinctive, I reserve the phrase "rules of the game" to a more limited set of rules than would Professor Cohen. I would argue that rules of the game are rules that parties in a particular setting generally observe and may feel a sense of obligation to observe, but do not have the quality of legal rules, moral rules, or rules of etiquette. These would indeed include informal agreements, gentlepersons's agreements, and tacit understandings.

Several concrete examples of such rules of the game can be given. As World War II was coming to an end, the war-time Allied leaders met in a series of conferences to decide the shape of post-war Europe. The declarations of Yalta, Potsdam, and Cairo produced arrangements that set the framework for European development after the war.[26] These agreements, however, were not codified in formal treaties. A similar kind of agreement was concluded thirty years later during the era of détente. In 1975, the Conference for Security and Cooperation in Europe convened in Helsinki for the purpose of drafting a new modus vivendi for East-West cooperation. The result was the Final Act of the Conference—what has come to be know as the Helsinki Accord. While this act contained provisions on human rights, reunification of families, scientific and technical cooperation, and other important issues, it was not a legally binding document. If one examines the statements made at the Conference, it is clear that the parties intended it to be something other than a formal treaty. President Gerald Ford, for example, noted that "the document I sign is neither a treaty nor is it legally binding on any particular state."[27] Nonetheless, the agreement was purported to be entered into in good faith and thus could be seen as imposing at the very least a "good faith" obligation on the parties if not a legal one.[28] Another example of rules of the game could be the way the superpowers behaved during the cold war.[29] There were a whole series of informal, implicit agreements between the United States and the Soviet Union. For example, both sides seemed to generally accept the notion that there should be no overt military intervention within each other's "sphere of influence." But once again, there was no sense of "legal obligation" (except as otherwise established) to adhere to this understanding.

This concept of rules of the game has been echoed recently in international legal scholarship in the notion of so-called soft law. In a variety of works, scholars have spoken about the "hard law"/"soft law" distinction. As Professor Paul Szasz explains, "hard law is, by definition, binding."[30] "By contrast," he explains, "soft international law is not binding, though superficially it may appear to be so."[31] According to Szasz, "soft law manifests itself in various ways."[32] He elaborates that "one is in hortatory rather than obligatory language contained in an otherwise binding instrument, such as in a treaty, when, for example, certain actions to be taken are introduced by 'should' rather than 'shall.'"[33] "More frequent," Szasz continues, "are obligations clearly expressed as such but set out in an instrument that is not binding, such as a resolution of an international organ or an agreement understood not to be considered as binding."[34] But, he adds, "such nonbinding 'precepts' (rather than 'obligations') are only to be considered soft law if international entities, particular states, habitually comply with them."[35] As Szasz sees it, "soft law is usually generated as a compro-

mise between those who wish a certain matter to be regulated defini-
tively and those who, while not denying the merits of the substantive
issue, do not wish to be bound by rigid and obligatory rules—perhaps
because they fear they cannot obtain any necessary domestic legislative approval."[36]

While this idea of soft law has received a great deal of scholarly
attention in recent years,[37] I find the use of the term quite troubling.
Due to its oxymoronic nature, it produces exactly the kind of impre-
cision that this chapter seeks to avoid. If a rule meets the criteria for
law, then it should be called "law." If, however, the rule is not binding—as soft law has been described to be—then it should not have
law anywhere in its name. If the rule is not obligatory, but is "habitually complied with," a "rule of the game" seems to be a much more
appropriate term. Given, in particular, the disdain with which international law is held by some international relations scholars, the concept of soft law seems to serve no purpose except to confuse matters
and dilute the distinctive nature of legal rules.[38]

A final type of rule can perhaps be termed "descriptive rules." A
descriptive rule is one that merely sets forth how "a group of people,
or most of them, behave 'as a rule' i.e. *generally*, in a specified similar
way in certain kinds of circumstances."[39] So, for example, people in a
particular community may all attend a concert each Saturday.[40] It could
thus be said that there is a "rule" that people behave this way. While
this notion of a descriptive rule is probably self-evident, it is useful to
mention since descriptive rules do exist and could be confused with
some other type of rule. In other words, an observer could note that
there was a certain type of regular behavior and erroneously conclude
that the existence of this descriptive rule meant something more. He
or she could conclude that regular attendance at the concert meant that
individuals were obligated to attend the concert. And while there certainly could be a rule that obligated persons to attend the concert, the
mere fact of their weekly attendance does not necessarily indicate that
there was an obligation. I believe that it is critically important, especially in examining international legal rules, not to allow practice
alone—the existence of a descriptive rule—to convince an observer
that a legal rule exists.

THE NATURE OF INTERNATIONAL
LEGAL RULES

Given this brief overview of rules in general, what can be said about international legal rules? What is international law? And is it really correct to call this international law "law"?

A Definition of International Law

Over the years, international law has been defined in a variety of ways. Drawing upon the general description of legal rules above, I believe that international law is most appropriately and accurately defined as *a set of legal rules that seek to regulate the behavior of international actors.*[41] In order to clarify this definition, I would make several observations.

First, international law is a set of *rules*. This may seem to be an unremarkable statement, especially given the previous discussion of rules. But a number of scholars have asserted that law consists of something other than rules. The adherents of the New Haven or Yale School, for example, contend that law is "process." It is a process of "authoritative decision." Echoing this view, Judge Rosalyn Higgins has recently submitted that "international law is not rules."[42] Rather law is a "specialized social process."[43] As Hedley Bull explains, those of the New Haven School "reject the idea of law as a 'body of rules' because they hold that this process of authoritative and effective decision-making does not consist simply of the application of a previously existing body of rules, but is shaped by social, moral and political considerations as well."[44] "The conception of law as a 'body of rules,'" Bull continues, "they see as one which restricts the scope of social, moral and political considerations in legal, and especially judicial, decision-making."[45] Undoubtedly, law is created through a process, and law can be changed through a process. And there is a distinct process of legal reasoning.[46] But "law" is not a process itself. To make law equal the process ignores that at a given point in time, certain concrete *rules* can be identified.[47] As Bull argues, "without reference to a body of rules the idea of law is quite unintelligible."[48] He explains that "if we are to recognise legal decision-making as a distinct social process and distinguish it from other processes of decision-making, it can only be by recognising that it is a process whose central and distinguishing feature is the attempt to shape decision in relation to an agreed body of legal rules."[49]

In a slightly different respect, writers of the "New Stream"[50] of international legal scholarship have also contended that law is not really rules in the conventional sense. According to Professor David Kennedy, law is not "a stable domain which *relates* in some complicated way *to* society or political economy or class structure."[51] Instead, law is "the practice and argument about the relationship between something posited as law and something posited as society."[52] As Nigel Purvis explains, according to New Stream adherents "international law is merely a particular type of discourse about international social life."[53] "It is," Purvis elaborates, "a method of conversation that states have chosen to follow."[54]

There is a sense in which I do not disagree with the New Stream characterization. The international legal process is indeed a form of discourse, a discourse manifested in both written and verbal communication, symbolic acts, and myriad other manifestations of state practice. For example, a state may make a verbal claim to a 200-nautical-mile territorial sea. Other states may then make verbal and written responses; still others may adopt domestic legislation on the matter; and still others yet may conduct freedom of navigation operations. Clearly, this is a type of discourse. The result of this discourse, I would argue, are legal "rules."[55]

In sum, I believe that the behavior of state officials and other participants in the international system clearly reflects the notion that these decision-makers believe that there are specific legal rules that can be determined. Law does not equal process; and even if it can be described a discourse, scholars can still identify specific rules at a given point in time.

Second, international legal rules are *legal* rules. What is commonly called international law is just as much "law" as domestic law. International legal rules are obligatory. They are rules that international actors are required to perform. International legal rules are produced through an international political process and are enforceable through that same process. They create an obligation that is owed to the international community. And the members of the international system regard the rules as *legally* obligatory. As noted above, these crucial characteristics differentiate *legal* rules from other types of rules. (More will be said about this issue in the next section.)

Third, in this definition I specifically note that international legal rules apply to *international actors*. Under traditional definitions, international law is said to regulate the behavior of *states*.[56] It is clear, however, that states are only one type of international actor that may be subject to international law. Other international actors include international organizations, "peoples," and individual human beings. International organizations may have extensive rights and duties under international law. They may enter into international agreements; their representatives may be entitled to immunity from jurisdiction; they may be able to bring claims against other international actors on behalf of their agents.[57] Similarly, "peoples" may have rights and duties under international law. While the word "people" is not extremely well defined, it seems to indicate a group that has a common ethnic, cultural, racial, religious, or linguistic identity. Under contemporary international law, "peoples" have the right to self-determination.[58] Finally, individuals may also be regulated by international law. For years, individual persons have been deemed to have certain duties under international law. It is illegal for a person to engage in piracy or slave trade or to commit genocide or war crimes. More recently, individuals have been seen as having rights under international law. Numerous treaties, including the International Covenant on Civil and Political Rights, seek to codify rights for individuals. It is thus clear that international legal rules now apply to a fairly wide-range of international actors, not only states.

IS INTERNATIONAL LAW REALLY "LAW"?

In the previous section, I have simply asserted that there are international legal rules—that there is international law. Yet, one of the most frequently discussed questions about international rules is precisely that issue: Is international law really law? Is it, in fact, proper to use the same term to describe certain types of rules on the international plane that one would use to describe rules in domestic political systems? In this section, I would like to examine this ontological question. To do so, I will first present some of the common arguments that suggest that international law is not properly called "law." Then, I will present several responses to these arguments.

Over the years, many arguments have been advanced attempting to deny the legal nature to international law. One of the most cleverly constructed arguments was presented (though not endorsed) by Professor Inis L. Claude, Jr.[59] In felicitous style, Claude explains that to many observers a rule can only qualify as a rule of law if it possesses the "Five C's": Congress, Code, Court, Cop, and Clink. First, the rule must be produced by a centralized legislative body—a "Congress," or parliament, or whatever. Second, this legislative body must produce a written "Code." Anyone should be able to pull out a statute book and read precisely what the rule says. Third, there must be a "Court"—a judicial body with complete compulsory jurisdiction to resolve disputes about the rules or to determine culpability for violation of the rules. Fourth, there must be a "Cop," some centralized means of enforcing violations of the rule. Finally, there has to be a "Clink." There must be some kind of sanction that will be imposed on those who choose to violate the rule.

If one examines the international system, it becomes clear that these "Five C's" are absent. First, there is no international "Congress." There is no international equivalent. Even though bodies like the United Nations exist, that organization has very, very limited legislative authority. Under the provisions of the United Nations Charter, resolutions of the General Assembly are not binding unless they deal with a limited set of internal matters such as admission of new members and the budget. And while the Security Council has the potential to adopt certain binding resolutions in matters dealing with international peace and security, this is not a true "legislative" authority in the general sense. The Council only deals with specific cases—such as the Iraqi invasion of Kuwait or the Indian and Pakistani nuclear detonations. It does not adopt broad, ominbus resolutions akin to legislative acts by a parliment. It would be wholly unprecedented for the Council to pass a resolution on the legality of intervention in general or the legality of nuclear tests in general. Second, much international law is not codified. As will be noted in subsequent chapters, a great deal of international law is created through "state practice." Rules of diplomatic immunity, to take but one example, existed for hundreds of years before ever being codified in treaty form. Third, there is no international "Court" with complete compulsory jurisdiction. To be sure, the International Court of Justice exists, and both it and its predecessor, the Permanent Court of International Justice, have decided many important cases. But cases only get to the International Court of Justice if states choose to take them there. Unless at some point states have consented to take a particular case or certain cases in general to the International Court, no decision can be rendered.[60] Fourth, there is also no international "Cop." In the post-cold war world, many might assert that the United Nations Security Council plays this role. There are, however, a number of difficulties with that argument. Under the U.N. Charter, the Security Council is not empowered to enforce *all* violations of international law.[61] Article 48 of the Charter provides that the Council can take action to enforce international law with respect to the maintenance of international peace and security. And Article 94 empowers the Council to take action to enforce decisions of the International Court of Justice. But there is no general right to enforce any other transgressions of international law. Finally, and following on this point, there is no guaranteed system of punishment—no international "Clink."

This argument seems to summarize most of the criticisms leveled against the contention that international law is really "law." At first examination, it appears to strike a very strong blow against international legal rules. I think the argument can essentially be broken down into three basic points: (1) the absence of a centralized legislature; (2) the lack of written laws; (3) the lack of enforcement (through adjudication and subsequent sanction). What can be the response to these three points? The first two contentions can, I believe, be fairly quickly disposed of. The third requires more careful consideration.

As noted earlier, law is the product of a political process. Typically, this process would take the form of some legislative body drafting written statutes. So, for example, the Congress of the United States adopts a new statute on the protection of the environment. But, as indicated above, in the Anglo-American tradition much law has developed without the participation of a legislative body. Common law rules emerged over the centuries through the practice of legal persons, judicial, and quasi-judicial bodies. In many of the states in the United

States today, certain crimes are still "common law" crimes and have not yet been codified in a state penal code. As a consequence, an argument that would reject legal status to international law because it was not created by an international "parliament" and put into written form would logically negate the legal status of much domestic law in common law countries. Practice and common sense, therefore, suggest that a "Congress" and a "Code" cannot be absolutely necessary conditions for a rule to be regarded as a *legal* rule.

But the real bane of international law has been the enforcement "problem." There is no international sanction that operates in the way sanctions operate in a domestic legal system. It was indeed this fact that caused John Austin to proclaim that there was no international *law*. Instead, what is commonly called "international law" was to him "positive international morality." Without a sanction, there could be no law. How have scholars responded to this problem?

One international legal scholar, Hans Kelsen, asserts that there is, in fact, a sanctioning process that operates at the international level. For Kelsen, a "rule of law" is "a hypothetical judgement according to which a coercive act, forcible interference in the sphere of a subject's interests, is attached as a consequence to certain conduct of that subject."[62] He explains that "the coercive measure which the rule of law provides as the consequence is the sanction."[63] The international legal order, according to Kelsen, is a decentralized, primitive legal order. Sanction does exist, but it takes the form of self-help. If a violation of a legal rule occurs (an international "delict"), states can undertake forcible reprisals to sanction the delictual behavior.

Professor Anthony D'Amato takes a similar, but slightly different, approach to the problem of enforcement. D'Amato claims that the sanction in international law lies in what he called a process of "reciprocal-entitlement violation."[64] International law, according to D'Amato, grants a series of entitlements to states—the right to territorial integrity, the right to claim a territorial sea, the right to diplomatic immunity, etc. When a state violates a rule of international law, the aggrieved state or states have the right to deny the recalcitrant state certain of its entitlements. To elaborate upon this point, D'Amato cites the example of the 1979 Iranian Hostage crisis. When Iran violated the diplomatic immunity of American embassy personnel, the United States froze Iranian assets. The United States responded in what D'Amato calls "tit-for-a-different-tat."[65] That is, rather than the United States responding in kind—that is, taking Iranian diplomats hostage—the United States denied Iran a different entitlement—the right to maintain fluid accounts in the United States. The freezing of these assets was met with at least tacit approval by the rest of the international community. Hence, D'Amato concludes, "the international community implicitly accepted the legality of a strategy that violates an offending nation's entitlements in order to repudiate that nation's initial offence."[66] This approach, D'Amato contends, is generalizable. As with Kelsen's approach, under D'Amato's understanding, international law is enforced in a decentralized fashion. Even though there are no centralized institutions for imposing sanctions, "the absence of these institutions does not mean that international law isn't really law; rather, it simply means that international law is enforced in a different way."[67]

For both Kelsen and D'Amato there is thus an international method of enforcing international law. They would say that there is, in effect, a "Cop" and a "Clink." Professor Thomas Franck, however, would respond differently. In his brilliant work, *The Power of Legitimacy Among Nations*, Franck wishes "to reserve the term *law* for describing a system of commands which, among its other obedience-inducing components, enjoys the contingent support of superior coercive power."[68] Despite D'Amato's attempt to find some decentralized sanctioning mechanism, Franck is not convinced. The international system is simply not like the domestic legal system. In a domestic system, centralized sanction is always one reason that actors obey law. This is not the case internationally. To cite an example, Franck compares the Internal Revenue Code and the Outer Space Treaty. He argues that "if nations carry out the strictures of the space treaty it is not due to fear of the enforcement power of some force or forces that are the functional equivalent of a global sovereign."[69] "That is not," Franck explains, "the sole or even *a* reason for their compliance."[70] Accordingly, Franck reaches the conclusion that at the international level there is "a system of rules which conduces to a fairly high level of perceived obligation among members of a voluntarist community."[71] These rules, however, are not really *law*.

While the efforts by Kelsen and D'Amato to find an international sanction are interesting and while Franck's attempt to bracket the ontological question is novel, both these approaches have difficulties. By making sanction a necessary condition for law, Kelsen and D'Amato would seem to do damage to domestic legal situations where no sanctions exist—for example, the *Steel Seizure* case scenario. Surely, the Supreme Court's decision had the force of law, even though no sanction could have been expected. Similarly, Professor Franck's approach is less than satisfying because it does not reflect the way international interactions take place.

Even though there is no centralized legislature to make the law, even though there is no guaranteed system of enforcement, international law is properly called law. Why? Like rules of domestic law, international legal rules are indeed produced through a political process and are enforceable through this process. Even though there is no absolute sanctioning system, there are certain possibilities for enforcing some rules through the Security Council, and there is a belief that it would be legitimate to impose sanctions for violating rules of international law. Finally, following Hedley Bull, I believe that the most important reason to consider certain international rules to be law is because international actors regard them as such. As Bull notes, "the activity of those who are concerned with international law, public and private— statesman and their legal advisers, national and international courts, and international assemblies—is carried on in terms of the assumption that the rules with which they are dealing are rules of law."[72]

Many concrete examples can be cited in support of this crucial proposition that certain international rules are perceived to be *law*. First, I believe it is abundantly clear that *states* regard these rules to be law. At the highest level, the constitutions of numerous states explicitly incorporate some notion of international law into their provisions. The Constitution of the United States, for example, empowers Congress to "define and punish . . . Offenses against the Law of Nations."[73] Article 25 of the Basic Law of the Federal Republic of Germany provides that "the general rules of public international law shall be an integral part of federal law."[74] The preamble to the Constitution of the Fourth Republic of France states that "the French Republic, faithful to its tradition, abides by rules of international law."[75] Similarly, the constitutions of Italy, Austria, and Greece all make explicit reference to international *law*.[76] At another level, the national laws of many states contain provisions that refer to international law. Moreover, as Bull notes, municipal courts in states throughout the world apply, at least in some circumstances, principles of international law to decide domestic cases. In other words, they operate on the assumption that these international rules that they are applying are legal rules. One of the most celebrated domestic court cases dealing with international legal rules is the *Paqueta Habana*. In that 1900 case, the United States Supreme Court pronounced that "international law is part of our law and must be ascertained and administered by the court of justice of appropriate jurisdiction as often as questions of right depending upon it are duly presented for their determination."[77] Moreover, when policy makers of a state act, they justify their actions in terms of international law. It is almost completely unheard of that a decision maker for a state would act in a controversial situation without attempting to justify his or her actions in accordance with international law.[78] While states may not always follow legal rules, the fact that they refer to these rules to explain their behavior indicates that they perceive legal rules to be of a different nature from other types of international rules. They perceive them to be *law* and thus to carry added weight as grounds for action.

Second, even other international actors regard these rules to be genuinely law. The decision-making elites of international organizations, from the United Nations to the European Union to various nongovernmental organizations make frequent reference to international law. Indeed, when the Secretary-General of the United Nations speaks, when a human rights group appeals to a state, they all refer to international "law." Virtually, all actors in the system behave with the understanding that the rules about which they speak are in fact law, not rules of the game or nonbinding moral norms. As Professor Bull asserts, "if the rights and duties asserted under these rules were believed to have the status merely of morality or of etiquette, this whole corpus of activity could not exist."[79] Bull explains that "the fact that these rules are believed to have the status of law, whatever theoretical difficulties it might involve, makes possible a corpus of international activity that plays an important part in the working of inter-

act as if law

national society."[80] In short, international actors call these rules "law," and act as though these rules are "law." Moreover, as the next chapter will demonstrate, even though the rules might be created differently from domestic law, they still have been constituted as "law" by the authoritative decision makers of the international system.

CONCLUSION

From the preceding discussion, it is clear that there are indeed a number of different types of rules that may operate at the international level. Despite the many scholarly understandings of the nature of these rules, I believe that legal rules form a distinctive type of rule. In order to appreciate contemporary international relations fully, it is necessary to understand that legal rules exist and that international actors regard them to have a different character than other types of rules. Even though these international legal rules may differ from domestic legal rules, they still have a decidedly "legal" character. As will be demonstrated in subsequent chapters, this character will have an important effect on the role these rules play in the international system.

NOTES

1. Chapter 4 will explore regime theory in greater depth.

2. Chapter 4 will also explore constructivism and the implications of this approach to international relations for international legal rules.

3. Stephen D. Krasner, Structural Causes and Regime Consequences: Regimes as Intervening Variables, 36 *International Organization* 1 (1982).

4. Id.

5. Id.

6. Id.

7. Id.

8. Professor Robert Keohane has explored some of the difficulties of differentiating "principles," "norms," and "rules." Robert O. Keohane, *After Hegemony: Cooperation and Discord in the World Political Economy* 57–61 (1984).

9. I realize that there are also many different definitions of the word "rule" itself. Professor Friedrich Kratochwill, for example, defines a rule as "a type

of directive that simplif[ies] choice-situtations by drawing attention to factors which an actor has to take into account." Friedrich V. Kratochwil, *Rules, Norms, and Decisions: On the Conditions of Practical and Legal Reasoning in International Relations and Domestic Affairs* 72 (1989). Professor Robert Keohane explains that "rules of a regime are difficult to distinguish from its norms; at the margin, they merge into one another. Rules, however, are more specific: they indicate in more detail the specific rights and obligations of members. Rules can be altered more easily than principles or norms, since there may be more than one set of rules that can attain a given set of purposes." Robert O. Keohane, *After Hegemony*, at 58. In the discussion that follows, I hope to clarify how I am using the word "rule." See also, Robert J. Beck, Anthony Clark Arend & Robert D. Vander Lugt, *International Rules: Approaches from International Law and International Relations* vii (1996) for a discussion of usages of the word "rule."

10. H. L. A. Hart, *The Concept of Law* 7 (2d ed. 1994).

11. I am indebted to Christopher M. Rossomondo for reminding me of this approach to moral rules.

12. In *The Abolition of Man*, C. S. Lewis reviews certain moral precepts that are common to world religious and philosophical traditions. C. S. Lewis, *The Abolition of Man* (1947).

13. See Samuel P. Huntington, The Clash of Civilizations?, 72 *Foreign Affairs* 22 (1993) for a discussion of competing philosophical frameworks.

14. See Fernando R. Tesón, International Obligation and the Theory of Hypothetical Consent, *Yale J. Int'l L.* 84 (1990).

15. See, for example, William V. O'Brien, *The Conduct of Just and Limited War* (1980) for an examination of the permissibility of force from a natural-law-based perspective.

16. I am indebted to John Russ for emphasizing this point.

17. Cicero, *On the Commonwealth* [*De Res Publica*] 215 (George Holland Sabine & Stanley Barney Smith trans., 1976).

18. Thomas Aquinas, *Summa Theologiae*, Question 91, A. Pegis (ed.), *Introduction to St. Thomas Aquinas* 616–627 (1948).

19. Question 91, in id. at 618.

20. H. L. A. Hart, *The Concept of Law*, at 8.

21. John Austin, Lecture 1, in *Lectures of Jurisprudence*, 86–103 (5th ed., Robert Campbell ed., 1972).

22. *Youngstown Sheet & Tube Co. v. Sawyer*, 343 U.S. 579 (1952). This case is frequently used by international legal scholars to argue for the efficacy of international law.

23. Professor Franck discusses the importance of legitimacy with respect

to international law. See, Thomas M. Franck, *The Power of Legitimacy Among Nations* 35 (1990).

24. Professor Anthony D'Amato seems to echo this important characteristic of legal rules. In a discussion of *opinio juris*, he notes that *opinio juris* means "articulation of a rule of international law." Anthony D'Amato, *The Concept of Custom in International Law* 76 (1971). One element of this articulation is that *"there must be a characterization of 'legality.'"* Id. He explains that "an explicit characterization enables states to distinguish legal actions from social habit, courtesy, comity, moral requirements, political expediency, plain 'usage,' or any other norm." Id. In presenting this point, D'Amato is implying that perceptions of "legality" play a critical role in distinguishing legal rules from other kinds of rules.

25. Raymond Cohen, *International Politics: The Rules of the Game* v (1981).

26. See Louis Henkin, Richard Pugh, Oscar Schachter & Hans Smit, *International Law: Cases and Materials* 147 (3d ed, 1993) for a discussion of these agreements and the Helsinki Final Act.

27. Statement of President Gerald R. Ford, 73 *Dep't of State Bull.* 204, 205 (1975), cited in *Frolova v. Union of Soviet Socialist Republics*, 761 F.2d 370 (7th Cir. 1985), reprinted in Thomas M. Franck & Michael J. Glennon, *Foreign Relations and National Security Law* 357, 361 (2d ed. 1993) (emphasis deleted).

28. Ford explained that "the Helsinki documents involve political and moral commitments aimed at lessening tension and opening further the lines of communication between the peoples of East and West." Id.

29. See Raymond Cohen, *International Politics*, at v.

30. Paul C. Szasz, General Law-Making Processes, in Christopher C. Joyner, ed., *The United Nations and International Law* 27, 32 (1997).

31. Id.

32. Id.

33. Id.

34. Id. at 32–33 (footnote omitted).

35. Id. at 33 (footnote omitted).

36. Id.

37. Id. at 32 n.6. Szasz cites a number of recent articles on "soft law." These include C. M. Chinkin, The Challenge of Soft Law: Development and Change in International Law, 38 *Int'l & Comp. L. Q.* 850–866 (1989). Recently, the American Society of International Law undertook a project to examine the nature of "soft law."

38. The conclusion that the term "soft law" is not very felicitous has been reflected in some very recent legal scholarship. See, for example, Jonathan I. Charney, Compliance with Soft Law, unpublished paper for the American

Society of International Law Soft Law Project. In his first footnote Charney explains that he "eschew[s] the term 'soft international law' or 'soft law' in favor of 'soft international norms' or 'soft norms.'" Id. at 1 n. 1. I am not sure that this is a tremendous advance, but it is certainly preferable to "soft law."

39. H. L. A. Hart, *The Concept of Law*, at 9. Interestingly enough, Hart refuses to call these "rules." Nonetheless, he captures clearly what I mean by "descriptive rules."

40. Id. at 9–10.

41. This definition is similar to that of Hedley Bull. He defines international law "as a body of rules which binds states and other agents in world politics in their relations with one another and is considered to have the status of law." Hedley Bull, *The Anarchical Society* 127 (1977).

42. Rosalyn Higgins, *Problems and Process: International Law and How We Use It* 1 (1994).

43. Id. at 2.

44. Hedley Bull, *The Anarchical Society*, at 128.

45. Id.

46. Id.

47. Presumably, the scholars of the New Haven School prefer to understand law as process in order to recognize the dynamic nature of law. They seem to believe that if "law" is conceived to be a set of rules, this dynamic nature is missed. I appreciate their desire to avoid thinking of law as a set of static, ossified rules. Law is dynamic. Nonetheless, law is not process itself.

48. Hedley Bull, *The Anarchical Society*, at 128.

49. Id. at 129.

50. On the "New Stream," see The New Stream, in Robert J. Beck, Anthony Clark Arend, Robert D. Vander Lugt, *International Rules*, at 227–229, 251–252.

51. David Kennedy, A New Stream of International Law Scholarship, 7 *Wis. Int'l L. J.* 1, 8 (1988).

52. Id.

53. Nigel Purvis, Critical Legal Studies in International Law, 32 *Harv. Int'l L. J.* 81, 115 (1991).

54. Id.

55. A New Stream scholar would probably contend that what I am calling "rules" are themselves a form of discourse and that this discourse is in constant flux. I still would not disagree. "Rules" are indeed a form of discourse and, as will be evident from chapter's 3 and 4, I believe they are in flux. But most rules have sufficient durability that a scholar can point to certain concrete rules at a given point in time.

56. Brierly, for example, defines international law "as the body of rules and principles of action which are binding upon civilized *states* in their relations with one another." J. L. Brierly, *The Law of Nations* 1 (6th Waldock ed., 1963) (emphasis added).

57. Louis Henkin, Richard Pugh, Oscar Schachter & Hans Smit, *International Law: Cases and Materials* 347–362 (3d ed. 1993).

58. The Charter of the United Nations makes reference to "self-determination of peoples." U.N. Charter, art. 1, para. 2 (1945).

59. To my knowledge, Professor Claude has never put this argument in writing. I draw upon numerous lectures given by him.

60. See Statute of the International Court of Justice, art. 36, for an examination of the jurisdiction of the Court.

61. Anthony D'Amato makes this point. Anthony A. D'Amato, *International Law: Process and Prospect* 9 (1987).

62. Hans Kelsen, *Law and Peace in International Relations* 29–30 (1942).

63. Id. at 30.

64. D'Amato, *International Law: Process and Prospect*, at 25.

65. Id. at 24.

66. Id. at 25.

67. Id. at 24–25.

68. Thomas M. Franck, *The Power of Legitimacy Among Nations*, at 35.

69. Id. at 35.

70. Id. at 35.

71. Id. at 40.

72. Hedley Bull, *The Anarchical Society*, at 136.

73. U.S. Constitution, art. 1, sec. 8.

74. Basic Law of the Federal Republic of Germany, art. 25, cited in Wildhaber & Breitenmoser, The Relationship between Customary International Law and Municipal Law in Western European Countries, excerpted in Louis Henkin, Richard Pugh, Oscar Schachter and Hans Smit, *International Law: Cases and Materials*, at 154.

75. Constitution of the Fourth Republic of October 27, 1946, preamble, para. 14, cited in id. at 156.

76. Wildhaber and Breitenmoser, The Relationship between Customary International Law and Municipal Law in Western European Countries, in id. at 145–157.

77. *The Paqueta Habana*, 175 U.S. 677 (1900).

78. I elaborate upon this point in more detail in chapter 4.

79. Hedley Bull, *The Anarchical Society*, at 136.

80. Id.

TWO

THE CREATION OF
INTERNATIONAL
LEGAL RULES

At every level, political systems have processes whereby legal rules are created. The city, the county, the province, and the state all have well-established and institutionalized mechanisms for developing legal rules. Likewise, over the centuries, an extremely sophisticated process has evolved for the formulation of international legal rules. What is this process? How do international legal rules develop? How does this process differ from the domestic legislative process?

The purpose of this chapter is to examine the process of creating international legal rules. In order to do this, the first section will set the stage by discussing the constitutive agents—those entities that create the legal rules. The second section will examine the traditional sources of international law. The third section will explore other possible sources of international law. Finally, the fourth section will examine the relationship among the sources. This examination, it is hoped, will provide the necessary foundation for an in-depth exploration of methods for determining international legal rules in chapter 3.

THE CONSTITUTIVE AGENTS

Many international legal texts begin with a discussion of the "sources" of international law—the ways in which legal rules are created. These works immediately delve into the international legislative process without first taking account of the nature of the international system itself. This approach is undoubtedly troubling to many international relations theorists. For them, it would seem impossible to understand how rules are produced unless the larger framework of international affairs is fully discussed. Different assumptions about the nature of international relations could clearly produce very different conclusions about the nature of legal rules and the role that they play in the system.

In fairness to international legal scholars, this failure to explore deeply the nature of the international system may be due less to a lack of rigor than to a long tradition of shared assumptions among legal scholars about the nature of the system. In the following discussion of the constitutive actors, many of these assumptions will become clear.

States

As noted in chapter 1, in most domestic legal systems, the primary means of creating legal rules[1] is through the actions of a centralized legislative body—a congress, a parliament, or even an individual "lawgiver." It is axiomatic to observe that there is no such body at the international level. As the structural realists observe, the international system is "anarchic," there is "no common power" to make the law.[2] Accordingly, most international legal scholars have asserted that in the decentralized international system, international law is created in a decentralized fashion by *states*. "States" thus make law.

The classic expression of this principle can be found in the *Lotus* case, which was decided by the Permanent Court of International Justice in 1927. In that case, the Court explained that "the rules of law binding upon States . . . emanate from their own free will as expressed in conventions or by usages generally accepted as expressing principles of law and established in order to regulate the relations between these co-existing independent communities or with a view to the achievement of common aims."[3] Thus, unlike domestic legal systems, "this means that states are at once the creators and the addressees of the norms of international law."[4]

The notion that states create law clearly proceeds from the realist assumption that states are the primary players in the international system, and that they act essentially as unitary actors. But while states are indeed the primary actors in the international system, states should not be thought of in a completely anthropomorphic fashion. "States" do not act; the decision-making elites in states act *on behalf of the state*. It is not Sierra Leone that agrees to a rule, but rather those individuals empowered to make decisions in Sierra Leone that agree to the rule. In reality, therefore, international law is created by the interactions of the decision-making elites of the states in the international system. By decision-making elites, I mean those individuals who are the effective decision-makers for the state. "Effective decision-makers" would be those officials of a state who are in control of the governmental mechanisms of the state, irrespective of whether they are perceived to be legitimate.[5] As a useful shorthand, however, it can be said that "states" create international law.

Nonstate Actors

As noted in the definition of international law provided in chapter 1, legal rules are binding not merely on the behavior of states, but also on the behavior of nonstate actors. A reasonable question to pose, therefore, is what role these nonstate actors play in the constitutive process of legal rules. If international legal rules apply to nonstate actors, do these actors help make these rules?

Under the present condition of the international system, I believe that nonstate actors generally do not participate *directly* in the law-creating process. Nonstate actors, with some exceptions that will be discussed below, do not interact with states in an unmediated manner. Nonstate actors may be the origins of a proposed legal rule, but in order for the proposal to become law, it must be accepted by states. For example, transnational environmental groups may formulate a proposed legal rule on ozone layer depletion. But this rule becomes international law only when *states* through their interactions make it law.

With the growing prominence of nonstate actors, it is possible that the international system may be moving toward one in which states would interact with nonstate actors directly in the law-creating process. At present, there are two notable exceptions to the notion that nonstate actors do not participate directly in the law-creating process: intergovernmental organizations and peoples.

Intergovernmental organizations are organizations the members of which are states—the United Nations, the Organization of American States, the International Atomic Energy Agency, and the like. In certain cases, these organizations have limited ability to enter into the law-creating process. This ability can be seen in two areas. First, intergovernmental organizations can in many cases conclude treaties. Thus, for example, the United States concluded the "Headquarters Agreement" with the United Nations to set forth the relationship between U.S. territorial jurisdiction and the rights of the United Nations. Second, some international organizations are empowered to enact resolutions that are binding on their members. The United Nations Security Council, for example, is authorized in certain circumstances to adopt decisions that are binding on members of the United Nations.[6] Similarly, various organs of other international organizations are able to make decisions that are binding on the member states.

In both these cases, however, the law-creating authority of the international organization results because states have vested this authority in the organization. International organizations can enter into international agreements because their framers intended them to be able to have that ability,[7] and certain organizations can adopt binding decisions because the members states have consented to that power. Intergovernmental organizations are thus not truly *independent* actors in the law-creating process.

A second type of nonstate actor that has recently been able to enter directly into the law-creating process are "peoples." As noted in chapter 1, the term "people" seems to mean a group that perceives itself to have a common bond based on a shared ethnic, cultural, racial, religious, or linguistic identity. Increasingly, the decision-making elites of certain "peoples" have been able to enter into international negotiations and conclude international agreements on behalf of their people. Hence, the Palestine Liberation Organization was able to conclude agreements with Israel to attempt to establish peace in the region. The Bosnian Serbs have entered into agreements with other parties in the Balkans.

Once again, however, the authority to conclude these agreements can be derived from the consent of states or an organization representing states. Moreover, the specific groups that have been empowered to conclude these agreements are still quite limited. "Peoples" in general have not been given a broad right to enter into the international law-creating process. In other words, except for the right of some groups to conclude agreements, they do not participate in the day-to-day interactions that give rise to general—global—international law.

As time passes, nonstate actors may continue to play a greater role in the law-creating process. If these trends continue, there may come a time when the international system will consist of both states and many other nonstate actors that will interact directly in making global international law. In fact, in chapter 5, I argue that these trends are moving in this direction. At present, however, states remain the fundamental law-creating agents.

TRADITIONAL SOURCES OF INTERNATIONAL LAW

If states create international law through their consent, how do they do so? What, in other words, are "the sources" of international law?[8] Even though virtually all basic international law texts begin with a discussion of the sources of international law, in order to appreciate various methods for determining rules of law, it is necessary to discuss briefly the traditional sources. Moreover, unlike some treatments of the sources of international law, this chapter argues that one particular source, "general principles of law," needs to be viewed in a new light. This source, it is argued here, in one of its forms, constitutes the very basis for the entire international legal system.

The typical starting place for a discussion of the sources of international law is Article 38 of the Statute of the International Court of

Justice.[9] Strictly speaking, this Article is merely an enumeration of the sources that the Court is to consult when attempting to determine the existence of a rule of international law for a pending case. In practice, however, scholars and decision-making elites nearly universally regard the sources listed in Article 38 as the authoritative delineation of the sources of international law.[10]

Article 38 lists three main sources of international law and two "subsidiary means for the determination of rules of law." The three main sources are international conventions, international custom, and general principles of law. The two subsidiary means are "judicial decisions" and the "teachings of the most highly qualified publicists of the various nations."

International Conventions

Conventions—treaties—are the most obvious, and perhaps the most maligned, source of international law. Treaties are formal, written agreements that spell out particular rules of behavior. Once a treaty has been signed, ratified, and entered into force, it is binding international law on all the parties. In essence, a treaty is the international equivalent of a contract; states consent to certain rules in a written document.

In the language of the discipline of international law, there are many different types of instruments that can be termed "treaties" or "international agreements." At the one end of the spectrum are bilateral treaties that establish rules for regulating the behavior of two states on a very specific issue for a very limited time period. An example would be a treaty between the United States and France on the exchange of a particular spy. At the other end of the spectrum are major multilateral agreements that establish complete governing regimes, such as the Charter of the United Nations or the 1982 Convention on the Law of the Sea. What makes both these kinds of agreements similar is that the rules they create, no matter how limited or how broad, are considered by states to be legally obligatory. The agreements do not merely establish "gentleperson's agreements" or informal arrangements; they establish law.

As just noted, treaties are the international equivalent of domestic contracts. They are not, however, the international equivalent of domestic statutes. Unless a treaty is ratified by all the states in the international system, it does not create "general" international law. That is, it does not create law that is binding on all members of the international system. This is not to say, as Professor Gerald Fitzmaurice does, that a treaty is not properly considered a "source" of international law.[11] Treaties are still sources of international law; they simply are not sources of "general" international law.[12]

Treaties may, however, codify a preexisting rule of customary international law. This occurs when a multilateral conference chooses to adopt a convention that incorporates established rules of customary international law. In such case, the convention may be cited as a shorthand notation for the general custom. So, for example, the 1982 Convention on the Law of the Sea could be cited to support the existence of a rule of general international law that allows for innocent passage through the territorial sea. The Convention did not create the right of innocent passage, it rather codified a rule of customary international law that had developed over the years.[13] Similarly, it is possible that a treaty may "crystalize" a rule of customary international law. Crystallization takes place when there is no preexisting rule of custom, but a multilateral conference reaches an international consensus on a new legal rule. This rule is then given written form in a multilateral convention. If authoritative state practice subsequent to the conclusion of the convention reflects that new rule, the convention can be cited as a shorthand for the new rule of custom that has been crystalized. In the *North Sea Continental Shelf* cases, the International Court of Justice suggested that it is possible for a multilateral convention to crystalize a rule in this fashion.[14]

Customary International Law

The second source listed in Article 38 is "international custom as evidence of a general practice accepted as law." Unlike with treaties, customary international law is not created by what states put down in writing but rather what they do in practice. A rule of customary international law develops when states behave in a particular manner and come to regard that behavior as required by law. In short, for a rule of customary international law to exist, two elements must be present. First, states must behave in a specific way; there must be a practice. Second, states must believe that the practice is required by law; they must believe that the practice is obligatory. In the traditional language of international law, there must be *opinio juris*. As Professor Schwarzenberger explains, "it is the subjects of international law [i.e., states] who are the sole law-creating agents, but the practice of one or several of them is at most an indication of what these subjects *consider* to be a general practice accepted as law."[15] "Only when all or most of them concur in viewing a particular practice in the same light, that is to say, accept it as law," he continues, "is an international custom transformed into international customary law."[16] Take, for example, the notion that diplomats enjoy immunity from criminal enforcement jurisdiction in their host state. This practice became a rule of customary international law as states began in fact to refrain from exercising criminal enforcement jurisdiction against diplomats *and* came to regard it as legally obligatory to refrain from exercising such jurisdiction.

Despite the less formal nature of customary international law, it is just as much "law" as are written treaties. As many commentators have noted, customary international law is analogous to common law in the Anglo-American tradition. Just as common law principles develop without a formal legislative act, so customary international law develops without formal codification.[17]

Because customary international law is by definition not manifested in written form, it can be much more difficult to determine the existence of a particular rule of custom. How can a scholar or a practitioner decide if a putative rule is truly reflected in practice and is accepted as law? More will be said about this problem in the next chapter. At present, however, it should be noted that in place of examining a single written text, an observer must look to find other indicators of practice and *opinio juris*. These include statements of governmental leaders and spokespersons, national legislation, domestic court decisions, behavior of governmental officials in particular cases, actions of diplomatic and military personnel, and a host of other examples of state behavior.

General Principles of Law

The third, and probably most imprecise, source of international law is what Article 38 rather anachronistically calls "general principles of law accepted by the civilized nations." There is a great deal of debate among scholars about what general principles are. In fact, some scholars would deny that general principles are really an independent source of international law. From an examination of the literature of general principles of law, there seem to be at least three plausible meanings of this phrase that are not necessarily mutually exclusive.[18] The first two meanings figure prominently in scholarship; the third is often overlooked, but, I argue, extremely important.

First, "general principles of law" may refer to general principles of law that are common to the domestic legal systems of states. In other words, if an individual were to examine the domestic law of states throughout the world, he or she would find that there are certain specific legal rules that are present in all or almost all of those domestic systems. One such rule might be estoppel. Estoppel is a legal doctrine that holds that when a party acts in a particular way and a second party relies on the act of the first party, the first party cannot subsequently behave in a manner contrary to its original act.[19] It is possible that an examination of all the world's legal systems would reveal that they have each adopted estoppel as a principle of domestic law. If this were found to be the case, it would be logical to assert that if a dispute arose between states, the principle of estoppel could be applied to that interstate dispute. If all, or virtually all, states had adopted this principle as a matter of domestic law, it could certainly be argued that they would accept it for international disputes, even though there may not have been an actual practice *among* states creating this principle as a matter of *customary* international law.

This interpretation of general principles has received wide support from decision-making elites in the international system and would seem to be an acceptable meaning of this provision of Article 38. In 1927, the Permanent Court of International Justice applied estoppel in the *Chorzow Factory* case—a dispute between Poland and Germany.[20] Two other general principles of domestic law that have been applied by adjudicatory decisions to international disputes are prescription and *res judicata*. Prescription is the notion that the passage of time can serve as a bar to bringing suit. In the *Gentini* case, a Mixed Claims Commission ruled that Italy could not bring a claim against Venezuela on behalf of an Italian national because too much time had lapsed.[21] The concept of *res judicata* was applied by the International Court of Justice in *Advisory Opinion, Effect of Awards of Compensation Made by the United Nations Administrative Tribunal* in 1954.[22] *Res judicata* is the legal doctrine that once a specific dispute between certain parties has been decided by a judicial body, and a final judgment rendered, courts will not adjudicate that same dispute again.[23] In the 1954 case, the International Court of Justice ruled that decisions made by the United Nations Administrative Tribunal were *res judicata* and thus binding on the parties.[24]

In light of the broad support for this interpretation, I believe that this concept of general principles reflects the consent of states in the international community. Nonetheless, it is not universally accepted. As Professor Schachter notes, "a significant minority of jurists holds that national law principles, even if found in most legal systems, cannot *ipso facto* be international law."[25] This is still, however, a "minority."

Second, some scholars would contend that general principles of law may refer to certain natural law principles. These scholars would submit that there are certain principles of "higher law" that are not created by consent proper.[26] Nonetheless, they would argue, these principles should be applied to disputes among states in certain cases. Two examples of such principles that are often cited are "equity"[27] and "humanity." The notion of equity has its roots in Aristotle's *Nicomachean Ethics*. In Book V of that work, Aristotle differentiates between law and equity. Law, explains Aristotle, consists of those rules that are meant to apply generally. The vast majority of the time, those rules will produce a fair and just result. In certain cases, however, legal rules will not result in a just result. Due to the peculiarities of some situations, applying law might cause an unfair outcome. It is in those cases that equity comes into play. Rules of equity constitute correctives against the absurd or unfair consequences of applying legal rules in certain cases.

Given this philosophical understanding of equity, some have suggested that notions of equity should be employed as a "principle of interpretation"[28] in disputes among states. In other words, they have argued that in court decisions, judges should use notions of "fairness" and "reasonableness" in deciding what the legal rule is. Equity is thus, as Professor Mark Janis notes, a "form of judicial discretion."[29] Other scholars have suggested that equity should be a "form of distributive justice."[30] Certain scholars from the developing world, for example, have argued that many so-called rules of international law—such as rules dealing with expropriation or other economic and resource concerns—are unjust. Accordingly, they believe that principles of justice should be applied to provide an equitable result.[31]

The concept of humanity works somewhat similarly. Here, the claim is that there are certain basic moral principles that can be translated into legal rules. A classic case where the International Court of Justice made reference to such principles was the *Corfu Channel* case. In that case, Albania had mined the Corfu Channel without providing notification of the location of the submarine mines. A British vessel navigating through the Channel was struck by a mine. Under conventional international law, the 1907 Hague Convention required states laying mines to provide notification of the locations of those mines, but this Convention only applied during time of war. Needless to say, there was no state of war at the time between the United Kingdom and Albania. As a consequence, the Court could not apply the provisions of the Hague Convention. Nonetheless, the Court concluded that the obligation to make notification of the locations of the mines was "based . . . not on the Hague Convention . . . but [in part] on certain elementary considerations of humanity, even more exacting in peace than in war."[32]

The difficulty with this understanding of general principles is that there do not seem to be universally accepted definitions of concepts such as equity and humanity. Rather, they seem merely to reflect subjective values espoused by certain states. From the perspective of the United States, for example, the Soviet Union may have violated the principle of humanity in shooting down the civilian Korean Airline flight 007 in 1983. The Soviets, however, probably did not believe that such a principle existed, let alone that they violated it.[33]

Third, general principles of law may refer to general principles about the *nature* of international law that are accepted by states.[34] Under this interpretation, general principles would refer to first principles about the international law-making process that are accepted by states. States, it could be contended, enter the international law-creating process with certain a priori assumptions. In order for the process by which customary international law and treaty law are created to make sense, states must first accept these basic principles. One such principle would be the notion that international law is created by the consent of states. For all the other sources to make any sense, it must first be accepted that states are the constitutive agents. Another such principle would be the concept of *pacta sunt servanda*—the notion that promises should be kept. Unless states have first accepted this principle, it would be impossible to regard any particular treaty as binding. Similarly, the notion that authoritative state practice even in the absence of a formal agreement—what we call customary international law—creates law would also be an a priori principle.[35] Finally, the notion that an existing rule of custom or even a provision of a treaty can be altered by subsequent practice would seem to be a first principle. Because all these principles are philosophically prior to custom and treaties, they can be regarded as separate sources of international law. States, for example, cannot by treaty establish the principle that treaties are binding.

Even though few scholars have *explicitly* recognized this interpretation,[36] I believe it is an important understanding of general principles. The other sources of international law are only comprehensible if states have previously accepted certain first principles about the nature of international law. As Professor Thomas M. Franck has observed in a related discussion, "it thus appears that the international community's capstone is the rule or set of rules defining formal sources of *obligation*."[37] This is exactly what rules like *pacta sunt servanda* or the notion that authoritative practice can create customary law do; they explain why other rules create obligation.

It is also significant to note that undergirding these general principles about the nature of international law are even more fundamental assumptions about the very nature of the international system. First, it is assumed that there is no centralized legislative body. For this description of the international law-making process to make sense, there can be no centralized legislative body. If there truly were such body, the sources of law would be quite different. Second, it is assumed that states are indeed the primary actors in the international system. Third, it is assumed that states are sovereign. In other words, it is assumed that states are juridically equal to one another and that they can be bound by no higher law without their consent. Hence, they *can* be bound by law with their consent.

Scholarly Writings and Judicial Decisions

— believes not independent ot int'l saves law

Finally, Article 38 lists the writings of scholars and court decisions as "subsidiary means for the determination of rules of law." Although there may be some debate on the question,[38] I believe that these two items are not independent sources of international law. Instead, they are things that a scholar or decision maker can consult in order to determine the existence of one of the three main sources. A scholar, for example, could examine court decisions and the writings of international legal scholars to assist in determining the content of a particular rule of custom, general principle, or the existence and meaning of a treaty. Courts and scholars do not "make" the law, but rather testify to its existence. Since it could be quite time consuming for each person seeking to identify a particular legal rule to undertake an independent assessment of state practice, it is often convenient to cite credible scholars and generally accepted court decisions that have already reaped the fruits of such an assessment. If, to take an illustration, a scholar or practitioner were seeking to understand the customary law concept of "military necessity," rather than exploring all the specific examples of state practice over the years, that individual may instead cite William V. O'Brien's classic article, "The Meaning of 'Military Necessity' in International Law,"[39] as a testimony to state practice in the period preceding its publication. Or, alternatively, if an investigator were attempting to determine international legal principles regarding "effective occupation" as a means of acquiring territory, he or she might choose to cite the *Island of Palmas*[40] case as an articulation of that principle.

use writing to articulate point to make law

OTHER POSSIBLE SOURCES OF
INTERNATIONAL LAW

International Organizations

With the increased prominence of international organization, much attention has been given to the role that international organizations play in the development of international law.[41] Indeed, a variety of scholars have been devoting a great deal of time to an examination of the law-creating function of international organizations.[42] Without attempting to catalogue the law-creating mechanisms of every international organization, this chapter will note two ways in which international organizations may create international legal rules: through binding resolutions and through the "special" character of United Nations General Assembly Resolutions.

1. Binding Resolutions

As noted earlier, some bodies of international organizations have the authority to create law that is binding on its member states. The most notable example is the United Nations Security Council. This general authority is provided for in Article 25 of the Charter of the United Nations. Under this provision, "the Members of the United Nations agree to accept and carry out the decisions of the Security Council in accordance with the present Charter."[43] Article 48 further specifies the requirement to follow decisions of the Security Council in matters relating to threats to the peace, breaches of the peace, and acts of aggression, noting that "the action required to carry out the decisions of the Security Council for the maintenance of international peace and security *shall be taken* by all the Members of the United Nations or by some of them, as the Security Council may determine."[44] Hence, when the Security Council adopted Resolution 661 following the Iraqi invasion of Kuwait in 1990, that resolution imposed a *legal* obligation on all members of the United Nations to impose economic and diplomatic sanctions on Iraq.

Under the Charter of the United Nations, resolutions of the General Assembly are for the most part only recommendations.[45] Some

General Assembly resolutions, however, are binding. These resolutions deal with such issues as financial contributions, budgetary matters,[46] and internal housekeeping and are binding on member states. These types of resolutions constitute what might be called "internal administrative law" for the United Nations.[47]

Similarly, bodies of other international organizations have also been empowered by their members to adopt binding resolutions. Organs of the World Trade Organization, the International Sea-Bed Authority, among others, have the authority to adopt binding decisions. At the regional level, the European Union possesses the ability to adopt certain types of legislative acts that are binding on the member states.[48] The Council of the European Union, and, in certain instances, the Council acting in conjunction with the European Parliament, can pass regulations, directives, and decisions.[49] These measures "are binding on the Member States, the Community Institutions and, in many cases, the citizens of the Member States."[50] The first type of legislative act, the regulation, "has a general scope, is binding in all its elements and is directly applicable in each Member State."[51] Moreover, "just like national law, it gives rise to rights and obligations directly applicable to the citizens of the European Union."[52] The next type of act, the directive, "binds any Member State to which it is addressed with regard to the result to be achieved, while leaving to national authorities jurisdiction as to the form and methods used."[53] Finally, "the decision is binding on the addressees it indicates, who may be one, several, or even all the Member States or one or more natural or legal persons."[54] What is thus most interesting about organs of the European Union is that they can create both legal rules that are binding on international actors (international law proper) and legal rules that are directly binding on actors *within* states.

2. *General Assembly Resolutions*

As noted above, certain General Assembly resolutions are binding on states. Some scholars, however, have contended that resolutions of the United Nations General Assembly may also have broader legal significance. There are at least two major claims about how these resolutions may have such legal consequences. First, General Assembly resolutions

Unanimous or partially indicates states regard it as law

Also other motivations for Gen. Assembly

are often cited as evidence of state practice. Some scholars contend that if a General Assembly resolution is adopted unanimously, or nearly unanimously, it indicates a belief on the part of states that the principles enunciated in the resolution are "regarded as law."[55] These individuals would, in consequence, be willing to rely on the resolution as the main indicator of state practice. Following other scholars and decision makers, I disagree with this interpretation.[56] I argue that states vote for United Nations General Assembly resolutions for a variety of reasons—to appease a domestic audience, to gain international acceptance, to gain specific favors from other states, and so forth. These reasons may have very little to do with the perception that the resolution should be regarded as indicative of state practice. I would contend that generally a General Assembly resolution should be regarded as but *one* possible indicator of a customary practice that should be taken into consideration along with the more traditional indicators— daily actions of states, statements of government officials, behavior of commanders in the field, and the like. It would be possible for a resolution to constitute a codification of existing customary international law. The resolution could thus be cited as a "shorthand" to denote the custom, much as treaties that codify customary international law are cited. To do this, however, it would be necessary to demonstrate that there was a rule of customary law that existed prior to the adoption of the resolution, and that the states adopting the resolution intended to codify this norm. Similarly, it would be possible for a resolution to crystalize a new rule of custom. But again, as with treaties, a scholar would have to demonstrate that subsequent state practice reflected this new rule in order for it to be regarded as law.

Interpretations of treaty for UN can make law

A second way in which General Assembly resolutions could be considered to have independent legal authority is as authoritative interpretations of the United Nations Charter.[57] Here the argument goes something likes this. The United Nations Charter is a treaty, and, therefore, binding international law. The General Assembly is a main deliberative organ of the United Nations. Thus, if the General Assembly adopts a resolution (again, unanimously or almost unanimously) that purports to interpret particular provisions of the Charter, that resolution should be regarded as *the* authoritative, and, therefore, binding interpretation of the Charter. In support of this argument, one could cite several decisions by the International Court of Justice. In the *Western Sahara* case, for example, the Court used several resolutions to assist it in interpreting Charter articles dealing with self-determination.[58] But once again, I would argue that even if a resolution were adopted unanimously, the Assembly is not explicitly given the power to render binding interpretation of the Charter. Only practice by states as reflected in the traditional ways in which state practice is assessed would be dispositive. The resolution could be one indication of that practice, it could codify a preexisting practice, or crystalize a new rule that would be confirmed in subsequent practice, but the resolution, in and of itself, could not be the binding interpretations of the Charter. Even though the International Court of Justice may have made use of General Assembly resolutions to aid in the interpretation of the Charter, the Court has never claimed that these resolutions alone are binding.

In sum, international organizations do have certain law-creating powers. Through binding resolutions, these organizations can impose legal obligations on their members. As noted before, this authority comes from the fact that states have given this power to the organization through the treaty—whether it be called a Charter, Protocol, Constitution, Covenant, or some other name—that established the institution. Accordingly, the ability of an international organization to create law is derivative of the right of states to adopt treaties. It should, however, be noted that international organizations do play another exceptionally important role in the process of creating law. In many areas—the environment, trade, human rights, and so on—nonbinding resolutions of international organizations begin a process that ultimately ends with the adoption of a treaty or the development of a rule of custom. The human rights area is an excellent example. On December 10, 1948, the United Nations General Assembly adopted the Universal Declaration of Human Rights. At the time of its adoption, the declaration was widely praised, but also acknowledged not to be a binding instrument. Nonetheless, the United Nations persisted in efforts to create binding instruments on human rights. Finally, in 1966, two covenants were produced—the Covenant on Civil and Political Rights and the Covenant on Economic, Social and Cultural Rights. These instruments were then sent out for ratification. As states have ratified these treaties, they have become treaty law for the signatories.

org. start process for law

Here, as in many other issue areas, an international organization played a critical role in beginning the process that resulted in the establishment of international legal rules.

Unilateral Declarations

Another way in which international legal rules may be created is through unilateral declarations. It is possible that a state may create legally binding rules through issuing unilateral statements that have the quality of law. This is the essence of the decision of the International Court of Justice in the 1974 *Nuclear Tests* case. The Court explained that "when it is the intention of the State making the declaration that it should become bound according to its terms, that intention confers on the declaration the character of a legal undertaking, the State being thenceforth legally required to follow a course of conduct consistent with the declaration."[59] While the Court acknowledged that not all unilateral declarations create law, if the state intends through its unilateral statement—whether expressed in writing or delivered orally—to establish a legal obligation, such an obligation is as binding as those established through treaty or custom.[60]

This method of creating international law may seem strange because it does not seem to involve the consent of more than one party. How can there be *inter*national law if there is only one state taking action? In practice, however, there really is more than one party. If a state makes a unilateral declaration, submitting that this constituted a legally binding pledge, even though other states did not necessarily accept the statement at the time it was made, when a second state challenges an action by the first state, claiming that the first state has violated its declaration, the second state has thereby accepted the legal authority of the declaration. It is analogous to one state drafting a treaty and then other states subsequently ratifying it.

THE RELATIONSHIP AMONG SOURCES

While the enumeration of the sources of international law provided in Article 38 is generally accepted as an authoritative listing, there is some disagreement about the relationship among the sources. What is the significance of the ordering of sources provided in the Statute of the International Court of Justice? Do some sources always take precedence over others? In examining the scholarship on these questions, there seem to be at least three possible positions. First, some scholars, such as Professor Prosper Weil, suggest that all sources are created equal. Weil explains that "the international normative system has traditionally been characterized by its unity: whatever their formal origins (custom or conventions, for example), whatever their object or importance, all norms [read—legal rules] are placed on the same plane, their interrelations ungoverned by any hierarchy, their breach giving rise to an international responsibility subject to one uniform regime."[61] Under this approach, if a situation arose where there were an irreconcilable conflict between a treaty and a rule of custom, the type of source would not determine how to resolve the dispute. In the event of such conflict the later in time—whether treaty, custom, or general principle—would prevail because the later in time is the most recent indicator of the will of the constitutive actors.

A second position is taken by scholars, such as Sir Hersh Lauterpacht, who suggest that there is some "priority"[62] to be assigned to treaties over other sources. He explains that "the rights and duties of States are determined in the first instance by their agreement as expressed in treaties—just as in the case of individuals their rights are specifically determined by any contract which is binding upon them."[63] Hence, he continues, "when a controversy arises between two or more States with regard to a matter regulated by a treaty, it is natural that the parties should invoke and that the adjudicating agency should apply, in first instance, the provisions of the treaty in question."[64] Customary international law takes second place: "It is only when there are no provisions of a treaty applicable to the situation that international customary law is, next in hierarchical order, properly resorted to."[65] Finally, "when neither customary nor conventional international law as formulated by treaty provides an answer that recourse may—and must—be had to the third, the residuary, source of international law, namely, 'general principles of law as recognized by the civilized States.'"[66]

Yet, it should be noted that Lauterpacht qualifies his understanding of this hierarchical relationship among the sources. He explains that the hierarchy "cannot be applied in a mechanical way,"[67] and notes that there may be some limitations on when a treaty will prevail over other sources. He explains that treaties may be, in fact, subordinate to certain higher principles: "As examples of treaties which may exceed the relevant limits, consider treaties providing for encroachments on the freedom of the high seas, or immoral treaties."[68] Nonetheless, these qualifications still seem to be derogations from Lauterpacht's basic hierarchy.

Finally, I offer a third approach. Drawing upon some of the insights of Professors Franck, Henkin and Schachter, I would propose two basic propositions for addressing the relationship among the sources. First, there is indeed a hierarchy of sorts—but one very different from Lauterpacht's. Second, outside of this hierarchy, there is equality among the sources.

As noted above, underlying the international legal system there are certain "general principles about the nature of international law." These are the a priori assumptions that form the basis for the other sources of international law. I assert that these principles are so fundamental to the entire enterprise that they must be given priority. That is, they would prevail over other rules of treaty, custom, or other types of general principles. The notion of *pacta sunt servanda*, for example, would always prevail over specific putative rules of custom or treaty.

At first glance, this approach would seem to contradict the proposition that law is created by consent. Could not states, through their consent, choose to supersede a general principle of this nature? There are several difficulties with that argument. First, these general principles have themselves been created through consent. They are the fundamental assumptions about the nature of the system that *states have made*. Second, these kinds of general principles are inherent in the very nature of the contemporary state system. If states choose to say that *pacta sunt servanda* is overturned—that promises need not be kept—the system is no longer recognizable. As Judge Hermann Mosler notes, "the law cannot recognize any act either of one member or of several members in concert, as being legally valid if it is directed against the very foundation of law."[69] Thus, these kinds of principles must prevail for the system to maintain its essential nature. Third, only very few general principles would fall into this category, which consists of only the most fundamental assumptions. Unlike Professor Schachter, who would place in this category such principles as "non-intervention, territorial integrity, [and] self-defense,"[70] I really believe that it must be strictly limited to those few essential principles.

Beyond these limited general principles, I would assert that all other sources enjoy the same normative weight. Accordingly, if a dispute arises and there is an irreconcilable conflict between two sources, the later in time will prevail. States can clearly choose to override an old rule by consenting to a new rule. The form this rule takes—treaty, custom, or general principle—does not matter. Because it is later in time, it is the authoritative expression of the consent of states.

CONCLUSION

The essential thesis of this chapter is that states create international legal rules through their consent. They express this consent primarily through the conclusion of conventions, through authoritative state practice, and through the acceptance of general principles of law. This basic assertion about the formulation of international law reflects a fundamental proposition of the "legal positivist" approach.[71] As Professor J. L. Brierly has explained, "the doctrine of positivism . . . teaches that international law is the sum of the rules by which states have *consented* to be bound, and that nothing can be law to which they have not consented."[72] This process of consent is the international political process that gives rise to international legal rules just as a domestic political process gives rise to domestic legal rules.

Although some scholars—such as Brierly[73]—would reject this fervent reliance on the doctrine of consent, I would submit that state consent is the most appropriate basis for explaining the creation of international legal rules. This is so because the positivistic concept of consent is consistent with certain basic understandings of the contemporary international system. International relations scholars ranging from structural realists such as Kenneth Waltz to constructivists such as Alexander Wendt have demonstrated that the international system is an anarchic system in which sovereign states are the primary actors. For there to be any legal rules, these rules must therefore be created by the states themselves. In today's international system, state consent continues to be the fundamental mechanism for generating legal rules.

NOTES

1. This is the *primary* means of creating law. In the Anglo-American legal tradition, common law, which develops through practice, is also an important means of creating law.

2. Professor Robert J. Lieber uses this expression from Thomas Hobbes's *Leviathan* as the title for his international relations text. Robert J. Lieber, *No Common Power* (3d ed. 1995).

3. *S.S. Lotus* (France v. Turkey), 1927 P.C.I.J. Ser. A, No. 10, reprinted in, Louis Henkin, Richard Pugh, Oscar Schachter & Hans Smit, eds., *International Law: Cases and Materials* 64 (3d ed. 1993).

4. Prosper Weil, Toward Relative Normativity in International Law?, 77 *Am. J. Int'l L.* 413, 420 (1983).

5. I am indebted to my colleague Robert J. Beck for emphasizing this point.

6. U.N. Charter, art. 25.

7. This is the principle upheld by the International Court of Justice in the *Reparations* case. *Reparations for Injuries Suffered in the Service of the United Nations*, 1949 I.C.J. 174.

8. Together with my colleague Robert J. Beck, I have set forth my understanding of the sources of international law in Anthony Clark Arend & Robert J. Beck, *International Law and the Use of Force: Beyond the UN Charter Paradigm* 5–10 (1993). This present discussion seeks to elaborate and expand upon that previous formulation.

9. Statute of the International Court of Justice, art. 38, para. 1.

10. Almost all international law texts and casebooks begin with this claim about Article 38. See, e.g., Malcolm N. Shaw, *International Law* 59 (3rd ed. 1991) ("Article 38(1) . . . is widely recognised as the most authoritative statement as to the sources of international law.") (footnote omitted).

11. Gerald Fitzmaurice, Some Problems Regarding the Formal Sources of International Law, in Von Asbeck et al. eds., *Symbolae Verzijl* 153, 157–158 (1958).

12. See Rosalyn Higgins, *Problems and Process: International Law and How We Use It* 33 (1994) for a discussion of this issue.

13. The right of innocent passage was also codified in the 1858 Convention on the Territorial Sea and Contiguous Zone.

14. *North Sea Continental Shelf Cases* (Fed. Rep. Ger. v. Den.) (Fed. Rep. Ger. v. Neth.), 1969 I.C.J. 3. In this case, however, the court held that a crystallization did not take place.

15. Georg Schwarzenberger, *The Inductive Approach to International Law* 19 (1965).

16. Id.

17. Frequently, rules of customary international law do receive codification. For example, the customary international law on diplomatic immunity was codified in 1961 in the Vienna Convention on Diplomatic Relations. These rules on immunity, however, were *law* long before their codification.

18. Oscar Schachter distinguishes among five different types of general principles. See Oscar Schachter, *International Law in Theory and Practice* 50–55 (1991), cited in Louis Henkin, Richard Crawford Pugh, Oscar Schachter, & Hans Smit, *International Law Cases and Materials* 104–199 (3rd ed. 1993).

19. *Black's Law Dictionary* notes, in part, that "'estoppel' means that a party is prevented by his own acts from claiming a right to detriment of other party who was entitled to rely on such conduct and has acted accordingly. . . . An estoppel arises when one is concluded and forbidden by law to speak against his own act or deed. . . . Estoppel is a bar or impediment which precludes allegation or denial of a certain fact or state of acts, in consequence of previous allegation or denial or conduct or admission, or in consequence of a final adjudication of the matter in a court of law." *Black's Law Dictionary* 494 (5th ed. 1979). I appreciate Robert D. Vander Lugt's help with this concept.

20. *Chorzow Factory Case* (German v. Poland), 1927 P.C.I.J., ser. A., No. 9, at 31.

21. *Gentini Case* (Italy v. Venezuela), Mixed Claims Commission, 1903, in Ralston, *Venezuelan Arbitrations of 1903* 720 (1904).

22. *Advisory Opinion, Effect of Awards of Compensation Made by the U.N. Administrative Tribunal*, 1954 I.C.J. 53.

23. Black's Law Dictionary defines *res judicata* as a "rule that a final judgement rendered by a court of competent jurisdiction on the merits is conclusive as to the rights of the parties and their privies, and, as to them, constitutes an absolute bar to a subsequent action involving the same claim, demand or cause of action." *Black's Law Dictionary* 1174 (5th ed. 1979) (case citation omitted).

24. *Advisory Opinion, Effect of Awards of Compensation Made by the U.N. Administrative Tribunal*, 1954 I.C.J. 53.

25. Oscar Schachter, *International Law in Theory and Practice*, cited in Louis Henkin, Richard Crawford Pugh, Oscar Schachter & Hans Smit, *International Law*, at 105.

26. Professors Henkin, Pugh, Schachter, and Smit discuss these principles of "higher law," citing "equity" and "humanity" as two plausible examples. Louis Henkin, Richard Crawford Pugh, Oscar Schachter & Hans Smit, *International Law*, at 113–119.

27. For an excellent discussion of equity, see Mark W. Janis, *An Introduction to International Law* 66–74 (2d ed. 1993).

28. Wolfgang Friedmann, *The Changing Structure of International Law* 197 (1964).

29. Mark W. Janis, *An Introduction to International Law*, at 66.

30. Id. at 74–79.

31. Id. See also M. Bedjaoui, *Towards a New International Economic Order* (1979); J. Singh, *A New International Economic Order: Toward a Fair Redistribution of the World's Resources* (1977).

32. *Corfu Channel Case* (U.K. v. Albania), 1949 I.C.J. 4, 22.

33. See John T. Phelps, Aerial Intrusions by Civil and Military Aircraft in Time of Peace, 107 *Mil. L. Rev.* 255 (1985) for an excellent discussion of the principle of humanity in this context.

34. Professor Schachter discusses something similar. He speaks of general principles "derived from the specific character of the international community." Schachter, *International Law in Theory and Practice*, at 104.

35. Thomas M. Franck, *The Power of Legitimacy Among Nations* 189 (1990).

36. Professor Thomas M. Franck has eloquently argued that there are certain fundamental a priori assumptions about the way in which international law is made that form the foundation of the modern international legal system. Although he does not specifically refer to these assumptions as "general principles of law," his analysis is very similar to mine. See Thomas M. Franck, *The Power of Legitimacy Among Nations*, at 183–194.

37. Id. at 190. (emphasis in original)

38. See Malcolm N. Shaw, *International Law*, at 59.

39. William V. O'Brien, The Meaning of "Military Necessity" in International Law, 1 *World Polity* 109 (1957).

40. *Island of Palmas Case* (U.S. v. Neth.), Permanent Court of Arbitration, 1928, 2 U.N. Rep. Int'l Arb. Awards 829.

41. M. Akehurst, *A Modern Introduction to International Law* 37 (5th ed. 1984). See also, Rosalyn Higgins, *The Development of International Law Through the Political Organs of the United Nations* (1963); Christopher C. Joyner, UN General Assembly Resolutions: Rethinking the Contemporary Dynamics of Norm-Creation, 11 *Calif. Western Int'l L. J.* 445 (1981).

42. Under the auspices of the American Society of International Law, a two-volume work was published: I–II Oscar Schachter & Christopher C. Joyner, eds, *United Nations Legal Order* (1995). An updated and abridged version was

published as Christopher C. Joyner, ed., *The United Nations and International Law* (1997).

43. U.N. Charter, art. 25.

44. Id., art. 48.

45. Id., art. 10.

46. Id., art. 17.

47. In a somewhat similar vein, Paul Szasz refers to "international administrative law." He explains that

> international administrative law is basically that which governs IGOs. Its principal manifestations are: the constitutional law of IGOs; procedural rules; the privileges and immunities of IGOs and their staffs; the rules governing the granting of assistance by IGOs to states; the rules governing various types of activities carried out by IGOs within states; and the personnel and financial regime of IGOs.

Paul Szasz, General Law-Making Processes, in *The United Nations and International Law*, at 32. He goes on to explain that "some of that law is created mostly by treaties; some by decisions of international organs; and some by the actions of these organizations, largely through their secretariats." Id.

48. This discussion of the European Union draws heavily upon Nicholas Moussis, *Handbook of the European Union* (2d rev. ed. 1995).

49. As Dr. Moussis explains, the Council "alone, in most cases, or with the European Parliament, in certain areas, adopts the instruments of secondary legislation on proposals from the Commission." Id. at 35 (footnote omitted).

50. Id. at 26.

51. Id.

52. Id.

53. Id.

54. Id.

55. See Richard Falk, On the Quasi-Legislative Competence of the General Assembly, 60 *Am. J. Int'l L.* 782 (1966); Samuel Bleicher, The Legal Significance of Re-Citation of General Assembly Resolutions, 63 *Am. J. Int'l L.* 444 (1969).

56. See the comments of a former legal counsel to the United Nations in E. Suy, *Innovations in International Law-Making Process* (1978), cited in Gerhard von Glahn, *Law Among Nations* 18–19 (5th ed. 1986).

57. This idea is raised by Henkin, Pugh, Schachter and Smit in their international law casebook. They note (but without providing the exact citation) that when the Charter was being written "a committee report noted that the

General Assembly was competent to interpret the Charter." Louis Henkin, Richard Crawford Pugh, Oscar Schachter & Hans Smit, *International Law* at 135. The Assembly had this power because (and here Henkin, et al. are quoting the report) it is "'inherent in the functioning of any body which operates under an instrument defining its functions and powers.'" Id. But the report "added that an interpretation of the Charter by the General Assembly would be binding on the members states if that interpretation 'was generally accepted.'" Id. Henkin and company go on to ask: "Does this mean that the adoption of an interpretive resolution by an unanimous vote (or near-unanimity) would be legally binding on the members?" Id. I would argue that "generally accepted" would mean accepted in *practice*. Thus, if subsequent state practice affirmed the interpretation given by the General Assembly, then it would be binding. But note, it is the customary practice that is affirming the law, not the vote on the resolution by itself.

58. This is discussed in id. at 133–136. See *Western Sahara Case*, 1975 I.C.J. 12 (advisory opinion).

59. *Nuclear Tests* (Australia & New Zealand v. France), 1974 I.C.J., para. 43.

60. Id. at paras. 44–46.

61. Prosper Weil, Toward Relative Normativity?, at 423.

62. Louis Henkin, Richard Crawford Pugh, Oscar Schachter & Hans Smit, *International Law*, at 94.

63. 1 Hersch Lauterpacht, *International Law: Collected Papers* 86–87 (1970).

64. Id.

65. Id. at 87.

66. Id. at 87–88.

67. Id. at 88.

68. Id. at 87 fn 1.

69. Hermann Mosler, *The International Society as Legal Community* 19–20 (1980).

70 Oscar Schachter, *International Law in Theory and Practice*, cited in Louis Henkin, Richard Crawford Pugh, Oscar Schachter, & Hans Smit, *International Law*, at 107.

71. Positivism as an approach to international legal rules will be explored extensively in the next chapter.

72. J. L. Brierly, *The Law of Nations* 31 (6th Waldock ed., 1963).

73. Id.

THREE

A METHODOLOGY
FOR DETERMINING
AN INTERNATIONAL
LEGAL RULE

The previous chapter examined the basic ways in which states create international legal rules. While there is general agreement about the primary means that states use to develop these rules, it is not always easy to determine when states have truly expressed their consent. Indeed, one of the most difficult and time-consuming tasks for contemporary scholars and government officials is to determine when a rule of international law exists. As Professor Weil explains, "the acts accomplished by subjects of international law are so diverse in character that it is no simple matter for a jurist to determine what may be called the normativity threshold: *i.e.*, the line of transition between the nonlegal and the legal, between what does not constitute a norm and what does."[1] Customary international law has always been quite elusive. When is there sufficient state practice? And when is there sufficient *opinio juris*? Similarly, general principles of law can be quite difficult to identify—especially since there is no common understanding of precisely what a general principle is. How do we know when the principle is truly "general"?

For treaty provisions, it would appear at first to be much easier to determine whether a legal rule existed. Professor Weil, for example, contends that "where conventional rules are concerned, the formality that presides over the conclusion of treaties and the principle of relative effect have enabled consensualism to be established without ambiguity or restriction: whether a state is committed by a treaty, and as from when, can be precisely ascertained."[2] Ideally, one would simply find the treaty provision and determine if a particular state were a party. If that state were a party, it would be bound by the provision. But, I would submit, it is not even that easy with treaties for at least two reasons. First, it can often be very difficult to determine the exact nature of the obligation contained in a particular treaty. Many significant legal debates have centered around the precise meaning of a treaty. During the 1980s, for example, there was a great controversy both within, and outside of, the Reagan administration about whether the development of a space-based ballistic missile defense system was prohibited under the Anti-Ballistic Missile Treaty. The applicable provisions of the treaty were sufficiently ambiguous to permit arguments on both sides of the question. And this is, of course, but one example. Very few treaties are without such ambiguities. Second, as I will argue below, the existence of a formal treaty provision—even if it is unambiguous—does not *necessarily* mean that there is a legal obligation. While the existence of a treaty provision does, I believe, constitute a prima facie case for the existence of a legal rule, it is not dispositive. This is a rather controversial position, but one that reflects the dynamic nature of international law.

In light of these challenges, the purpose of this chapter is to propose a methodology for determining the existence of a rule of international law. It proceeds from the legal positivist assumption that international legal rules are created by the consent of states. Accordingly, it seeks to provide guidelines that scholars, officials, and others can use to determine when this consent has been given. In order to accomplish this task, this chapter is divided into three sections. The first section will examine several existing methodologies that have been developed to deal with this issue. The second section will set forth my methodology. The third section will conclude the chapter.

EXISTING METHODOLOGIES

When natural law dominated international jurisprudence, the method most often employed by those seeking to determine if a rule of international law existed is what might be called "deductive."[3] The great scholastic writers, such as Francisco Suarez and Francisco Vitoria, deduced particular legal rules from basic natural law propositions. In their examinations of the laws of warfare, for example, these writers drew on Hebrew and Christian Scripture, theological treatises, classical philosophy, and even mythology, to establish certain truths that could then be translated into specific rules for the conduct of war.[4]

With the emergence of the modern state system in the seventeenth century, scholars began to move away from a primarily deductive approach. As states came to be regarded as the creators of international legal rules, writers began to introduce "inductive" methods into their scholarship. While "some of the early positivists still vacillated between the traditional [deductive] approach and the newly-discovered truth that international law was the sum total of the rules actually considered law by the subjects of international law,"[5] positivism as it developed became essentially inductive. Positivists, in their quest to find rules of international law, looked at the "raw data,"[6] at state practice. From this practice, they would then induce the legal rules. A positivist scholar would, for example, engage in an exhaustive examination of state behavior relating to jurisdictional claims to the sea, before concluding that a particular jurisdictional zone was established under international law.

Throughout the twentieth century, this positivist inductive approach has predominated. Scholars, ranging from Georg Schwarzenberger to Lassa Oppenheim to C. Wilfred Jenks to Prosper Weil, have used some version of the positivist method to provide their assessment of the rules of international law. Nonetheless, since the mid-century, a slightly different method has played an important role in international legal scholarship. Beginning in the 1950s with monumental works by Myres McDougal and Harold Lasswell of Yale, the New Haven School has gained many adherents. Such distinguished scholars as Myres McDougal, W. Michael Reisman, John Norton Moore, Richard Falk,

Florentino Feliciano, and Rosalyn Higgins have written extensively using the methodology of the New Haven School. The New Haven approach draws on many of the insights of positivism, but, as will be discussed below, uses new concepts and some deductive methods in the process of determining rules of international law.

While there are perhaps as many different international legal methodologies as there are scholars, this section will explore traditional positivism and the New Haven school as examples of two of the most prominent of the current methodologies. It will lay out the basic contours of these two approaches and provide a critique of them. This examination will then set the stage for the explication of a new methodology.

Traditional Positivism

As noted above, traditional positivism teaches that international law is created through state practice. Accordingly, an inductive method is used to determine the nature of legal rules. In setting forth his inductive approach, Professor Schwarzenberger explains that this approach places "emphasis on the working hypothesis—historical research and the near-universality of Article 38 of the Statute of the World Court tend to transform it into a certainty—of the exclusive character of the three law-creating processes in international law: consensual understandings in the widest sense, international customary law, and the general principles of law recognised by civilized nations."[7] Under positivism, the scholar discovers rules of law by determining what states have consented to through these sources. As Professors McDougal, Lasswell, and Reisman have explained, in a positivist world, "the jurist is regarded as neither authorized nor qualified seriously to consider the social context in which rules are generated or the socio-political consequences which rules, in turn, engender in specific instances of application."[8] In other words, the positivist scholar is not to examine the context or to consider broader goals or purposes of the international political system in determining specific rules. He or she is not to impose a particular teleology on the law-finding task. The law is what states have created. If on a particular issue there is no rule of international law, the scholar is not to fill the "gap" by reference to these other goals. As Professor Kelsen notes, "if there is no norm of conventional or customary international law imposing upon the state (or other subject of international law) the obligation to behave in a certain way, the subject is under international law legally free to behave as it pleases."[9]

How does this approach translate into a concrete method for dealing with the three basic sources of international law? With respect to treaties, positivists typically assert legal rules can be found by consulting provisions of treaties that have entered into force. Among these scholars, there seems to be a great deal of sanctity accorded to the written text. The treaty is the law. Although even positivist writers may assert that "immoral treaties"[10] are not valid, they generally express great skepticism about treaties being superseded or altered by anything other than another treaty. Hans Kelsen, for example, has grave reservations about the entire concept of *rebus sic stantibus*—the notion that treaties can be terminated when a "fundamental change of circumstances" takes place.[11] He explains "that it is the function of the law in general and treaties in particular to stabilize the legal relations between states in the stream of changing circumstances."[12] "If circumstances did not change," he continues, "the binding force conferred upon treaties by the law would be almost superfluous."[13] Moreover, "the relatively few cases in which states have referred to essential change of circumstances to justify their noncompliance with treaty obligations may be interpreted simply as violations of international law rather than evidence of the *clausula rebus sic stantibus*."[14] "As a matter of fact," Kelsen concludes, "no international tribunal has, until now [1952], unreservedly confirmed the existence of this rule [*rebus sic stantibus*]."[15]

More recently, another contemporary positivist, Professor Prosper Weil, has expressed concerns about the concept of *jus cogens*—the notion that there are certain "peremptory" rules of international law and that treaties cannot be concluded that violate these rules. The theory of *jus cogens* works something like this: If, for example, a *jus cogens* existed that prohibited states from engaging in slave trade, they could not by treaty consent to undertake that behavior; such treaty would be void and thus without legal effect. For Professor Weil, the concept of *jus cogens* creates difficulties for the basic positivist notion of the equality of all rules—whatever their source. He explains that "one can scarcely overemphasize the uncertainties inflicted on the international normative system by the fragmentation of normativity that the theories of *jus cogens* and international crimes have brought in their wake."[16] How does one determine whether a rule is a *jus cogens* or merely an ordinary rule of international law?[17] Moreover, if distinctions can be drawn between regular legal rules and superrules, what is to prevent even more specific normative gradations?[18] "A normativity subject to unlimited gradation is," in his opinion, "one doomed to flabbiness, one that in the end will be reduced to a convenient term of art, covering a great variety of realities difficult to grasp."[19] Like Kelsen, Weil is very skeptical about doctrines that would interfere with the basic proposition that states can establish whatever law they wish through treaties.

To a positivist scholar, therefore, one bit of "raw evidence" of legal rules is a treaty. It is a primary way in which states consent. If a treaty exists on a particular issue and a state is a party to a treaty, that written document almost certainly establishes legal rules binding on the state.

With customary international law, positivists have developed an extremely involved method for finding consent in the vicissitudes of state practice. Consistent with a general understanding of the sources of international law discussed in the previous chapter, positivists contend that both the "objective" and the "subjective" elements of custom must be present in order for there to be a rule of customary international law. First, there must be physical practice. States must engage in some activity. They must arrest fishing vessels; or they must refrain from arresting fishing vessels. They must grant immunity from criminal jurisdiction; or they must refuse to grant immunity from criminal jurisdiction. This is the objective element. It is what states do in practice. Second, there must be *opinio juris*. The practice in which the states engage must be regarded as law. This is the subjective element.

To determine the existence of these two elements, positivists consult a wide array of data. Indeed, any international law textbook or casebook contains a recitation of the kinds of evidence scholars of positivism and other persuasions would muster to determine the existence of a rule of custom. Such a listing, as observed in the previous chapter, could include statements by government officials, actions and decisions taken by government officials, domestic legislation, activities of diplomatic personnel, behavior of military commanders, decisions of domestic courts, and the like. But how does the observer evaluate this data? How does one measure practice and *opinio juris*? Professor Weil, noting that "it is not always easy to draw the frontier between the prelegal and the legal,"[20] cites Justice Stuart's famous comment about pornography—"I know it when I see it." Explains Weil: "this celebrated formula of a Justice of the United States Supreme Court aptly illustrated this difficulty."[21]

Positivists typically provide a variety of guidelines to assist the observer in evaluating the status of putative legal rules. They generally begin with the assertion that there must be a long, well-established, nearly universal practice of states. Sir Hersch Lauterpacht, himself not a strict positivist,[22] expresses this point nonetheless. As he notes, "international custom signifies constant and uniform practice followed by States as a matter of obligation."[23] Similarly, Kelsen explains that "custom is a usual or habitual course of action, a long-established practice; in international relations, a long-established practice of states."[24] Hence, a scholar operating under the traditional approach would first attempt to find a practice that was consistent. Day after day, year after year, states would have to engage in the practice. They would, for example, have to consistently refrain from shooting prisoners of war, or from denying foreign vessels transit through international straits. Second, the scholar would determine that the practice was nearly universal. Most positivists would assert that not all states need participate or acquiesce in a practice, but there should be near uniformity. These positivist guidelines are, of course, still quite vague. As Lauterpacht notes, "constancy and uniformity of practice are a matter of degree."[25] "There is," Lauterpacht explains, "no rule of thumb which renders it possible to predict with any degree of assurance what amount of precedent will cause an international tribunal to assume in any given case that the degree of accumulation of precedent qualifies as custom."[26]

Finally, traditional positivists seem to have some difficulties with the third formal source of international law—general principles of law. It is remarkable that in his 1952 treatise entitled *Principles of International Law*, Professor Kelsen does not even discuss general principles as a source of international law. In his chapter on "The Creation (Sources) of International Law," Kelsen declares that "the two principal methods of creating international law are custom and treaties."[27] He then devotes two long sections in the text to each of those methods, but only discusses "general principles" in a passing comment about the International Court of Justice.[28] Later, he contends that "it is doubtful whether such principles common to the legal orders of the civilized nations exist at all."[29] He further notes that "Article 38, paragraph 1 [of the Statute of the International Court of Justice], expressly stipulates that the function of the Court is 'to decide in accordance with international law.'"[30] "Hence," he continues, "it might be argued that 'the general principles of law' are applicable only if they are part of international law, and that means part of the law referred to in clauses (a) [conventions] and (b) [custom] of Article 38."[31] If this is the case, "clause (c) [general principles] is superfluous."[32] In short, for general principles to be part of international law, these principles must have been enacted through either treaties or custom. They do not, under Kelsen's positivism, seem to be an independent source of legal rules.

Other positivists are not as ardent in their rejection of general principles. While they do not generally acknowledge any notion of general principles that involves concepts of higher law, such as those of equity and humanity, some positivists accept the notion that common principles of municipal law may be a source of international law. Professor Schwarzenberger, for example, supports this understanding of general principles. He approvingly cites a test for determining the existence of such principles developed by H. C. Gutteridge: "If any real meaning is to be given to the words 'general' or 'universal' and the like, the correct test would seem to be that an international judge before taking over a principle from private law must satisfy himself that it is recognised in substance by all the main systems of law and that in applying it he will not be doing violence to the fundamental concepts of any of those systems."[33] In other words, for a rule to be regarded as a general principle, a survey of the world's major legal systems must take place. If the principle is found in civil law systems, common law systems, and all other different legal systems that may exist, the principle can be applied to interstate cases.

Traditional Positivism: A Critique

Traditional positivism has much to commend itself as a useful methodology for determining legal rules. It recognizes the anarchic nature of the international system and accepts states as the creators of international legal rules. It draws a fairly clear distinction between legal rules and moral rules. While not denying the existence of moral rules, positivist scholars, unlike natural law writers, refrain from conflating the two types of rules. There are, however, a number of difficulties with the traditional positivist approach.

First, positivism tends to place too much emphasis on the absolute sanctity of treaties. While undoubtedly treaties create law among states, the international law-creating process remains dynamic. As noted earlier, I believe the existence of a treaty is prima facie evidence of a rule of law. But states can choose to alter legal rules established by treaty through customary practice. A concrete example can serve to illustrate this point. Article 2(4) of the United Nations Charter prohibits "the threat or use of force against the territorial integrity or political independence of any state or in any other manner inconsistent with the Purposes of the United Nations."[34] This provision has not been formally changed by amendment; nor has any state *formally* invoked the doctrine of *rebus sic stantibus* as provided for in the Vienna Convention on the Law of Treaties. Nonetheless, as Professor Robert Beck and I have argued elsewhere,[35] through customary practice, states have effectively withdrawn their consent from this provision. In their practice, states do not refrain from such uses of force, and they no longer truly accept the provision as law. Many positivists would assert that the mere existence of the U.N. Charter provision is sufficient to demonstrate that Article 2(4) is reflective of a legal rule. The Charter is, after all, still in force as a multilateral treaty.[36] This claim, I believe, denies the right of states to withdraw their consent through custom and thus denies the dynamic nature of international law.

Second, positivism tends to underrate the role of general principles of law. In particular, positivists do not generally acknowledge the notion of general principles about the nature of international law. These principles, as noted in the previous chapter, undergird the international legal system. They are still created by consent because they form the shared a priori assumptions of states—the primary international actors. Most positivists acknowledge principles such as *pacta sunt servanda*, but they tend to think of these principles as something other than consent-created general principles.

Third, the positivist methodology for determining the existence of legal rules is rather vague. As noted above, many positivists recognize how difficult it is using this methodology to verify the existence of a legal rule. The notion that the observer would "know it when he or she saw it" is not particularly easy to operationalize. Perhaps this will always remain a major stumbling block in the development of a methodology for determining legal rules. But perhaps it may be possible to formulate more specific guidelines that will provide greater assistance to scholars, officials, and others seeking to find rules of international law.

The New Haven Approach

In the post-World War II era, the major challenge to positivism in international legal theory has come from the McDougal-Lasswell school of jurisprudence. Despite arguments by some that this method has become passé,[37] a substantial number of legal scholars throughout the world have been greatly influenced by the theories of Myres McDougal, Harold Lasswell, and their students.[38] In their writings, those of the New Haven School have provided a new definition of law and have elaborated a very detailed methodology for use in determining the law. While it would be impossible to do justice to this approach in a few pages, the following material will attempt to set out the most basic contours of this approach.

As noted earlier, adherents of the New Haven School define law not as a set of rules but as a particular kind of social process. To be specific, they define law as the process of "authoritative decision." According to this approach, the world can be understood in terms of a series of overlapping social processes. At the broadest level is what McDougal and Lasswell call the "world social process."[39] The world social process is a process of interaction consisting of human beings "acting individually in their own behalf and in concert with others with

whom they share symbols of common identity and ways of life of varying degrees of elaboration."[40] The purpose of this process is "the
maximization of values within the limits of capability."[41] "A value,"
they explain, "is a preferred event."[42] It is, thus, whatever individuals
desire. Since a complete list of all conceivable values is impossible,
McDougal and Lasswell believe that most values can be understood
as falling into one or more of the following categories: health, safety,
comfort (well-being), affection, respect, skill, enlightenment, rectitude,
wealth, and power.[43] In other words, human beings seek a variety of
values that aim at achieving skill or power or affection and so on.

Operating within this broad social process is yet another process—
what McDougal and company refer to as the "world power process."[44]
The world power process is the process by which certain values are
actually realized in the world. In other words, this is the process that
determines specific "outcomes"—what really happens, who gets what.
From this process come decisions that control behavior—whether or
not those decisions are perceived to be legitimate or not. For example,
during the period of Western colonization, the world power process
led to the Western states gaining control over much of the developing
world. It was the Western states who had the resources—military
might, economic wealth, etc. As a consequence, as these states interacted with less resourceful political units in the system, these Western
states were able to realize their values.

Finally, within the world power process is the legal process. This
process McDougal and Lasswell define as "the making of authoritative and controlling decisions."[45] With this phrase, they introduce the
two most critical concepts for understanding law under their framework: authority and control. They define "authority" as "the structure of expectation concerning who, with what qualifications and mode
of selection, is competent to make which decisions by what criteria
and what procedures."[46] Professor John Norton Moore explains this
a bit more clearly. In a 1968 law review article entitled "Prolegomenon
to the Jurisprudence of Myres McDougal and Harold Lasswell," he
explains that authority "is used to signify community expectations
about how decisions should be made and about which established
community decision-makers should make them."[47] As a consequence,
"decisions made in conformance with community expectations about

proper decision and proper decision-makers, as distinguished from decisions based on mere naked power, are said to be authoritative."[48]

In essence, a decision is authoritative if "the members of the community" perceive the decision to be made in a legitimate manner, irrespective of whether it actually controls behavior. A few examples may illustrate. If the Congress of the United States passes a tax bill and the president signs the bill, that act is generally perceived to be authoritative by the citizens of the United States. People believe that Congress and the president had the authority to undertake this action. Similarly, if a treaty concerning the prohibition on torture is concluded and ratified by a number of states but ignored by most of them, the procedure is regarded as authoritative, even if the treaty did not control behavior.

As can be seen, the concept of authority seems to be similar to the traditional notion of *opinio juris*. There do, however, seem to be distinctions. One will be noted here; the other will be discussed later in this section.

In a typical positivist approach, when scholars ask if a rule has *opinio juris*, they are asking if that rule is perceived to be law. In the New Haven approach, scholars seem to ask something else. The McDougalian scholars want to know if the *process* whereby a decision is made is perceived to be legitimate. They ask if the decision was made by legitimate decision makers through a legitimate process. If the decision was so made, then it has authority. Herein lies the distinction. As noted earlier, positivists contend that law consists of *rules*. Accordingly, they are first and foremost concerned about whether the *rule* itself is perceived to be law. Generally speaking, of course, a rule that is produced through a legitimate process will be perceived to be legitimate. But it is certainly possible that a rule could emerge through a less than legitimate process that, over time, would nonetheless come to be perceived to be the law.[49] Similarly, it is possible that a rule could be produced through a legitimate process but come to be perceived to no longer be the law. Positivists are not primarily interested in the legitimacy of the process—although that would certainly provide important data—but rather in the legitimacy of the result.

The other element of the legal process according to the New Haven approach, "control" is defined as "an effective voice in decision, whether authorized or not."[50] A decision is controlling if it determines an actual outcome, irrespective of whether or not it was perceived to be authoritative. So, to take the previous example, if individuals pay the amount of tax prescribed in legislation, that action by Congress and the president was controlling. If, however, the legislation is widely ignored by the populace, it is not controlling, even though it may have been authoritative. In the international arena, there are a plethora of controlling events that are not authoritative. When China suppressed the Tiananmen Square demonstration or the United States invaded Panama, these acts were ultimately controlling, yet many perceived them to be made through an illegitimate process—not authoritative.

Using these two concepts, the members of the New Haven School can thus define law: "The conjunction of common expectations concerning authority with a high degree of corroboration in actual operation is what we understand by law."[51] Hence, the process that produces decisions that are both authoritative and controlling is the legal process. McDougal, Lasswell, and Reisman explain that "an authoritative and controlling decision can be contrasted with decisions involving only effective power ('naked power') or mere barren authority ('pretended power')."[52] They then proceed to give examples of these two extremes. They see "'naked power' in action when a strong empire coerces a weak neighboring polity, and nothing happens [i.e., the international community as a whole does not respond]."[53] "Pretended power" they find in a situation "when a superseded monarch vainly claims acceptance as the legitimate head of the body-politic from which he has been expelled."[54]

With this understanding of law as the conjunction of authority and control, McDougal and colleagues can explain their method for determining the existence of international law. In order to examine this method, it is necessary to explore their answers to four specific questions. First, whose expectations of authority are to be sought? Second, how does an observer "measure" authority and control? Third, how much authority and control are necessary for "law" to exist? Fourth, are there factors other than authority and control that are involved in the law-determining process?

As noted earlier, authority in the New Haven formulation is somewhat different from *opinio juris*. In addition to the difference noted above, there is at least one more distinction. For positivists, it is the perceptions of *states* that is used to determine *opinio juris*. For those of the New Haven School, the perceptions of authority come from a broader group. McDougal, Lasswell, and Reisman explain that "authority will be sought, not in some mysterious or transempirical source of 'obligation' or 'validity,' but rather, empirically, in the perspectives, the genuine expectations, of the people who constitute a given community about the requirements for lawful decision in that community."[55] It is thus the expectations of "the people" of the "community" that are used to determine whether something is authoritative, not those of the "state." Elsewhere, the authors explain that "in the optimum public order which we recommend, the expectations of *all individuals equally* comprise authority."[56] But recognizing that in contemporary "public order systems, full universality and democracy are rarely achieved," they assert that "the expectations and demands of the effective elites of a polity may be the dominant element of authority in a particular community."[57] In other words, given the current status of developments in the global system, it is too early to examine the expectations of *all* human beings. At present, therefore, a scholar seeking to explore perceptions of authority should look at the expectations of "effective elites." But who are these effective elites? Are these the decision-making elites that are empowered by the people of states to act on their behalf? Or is this a broader category of elites? Is this a category that might include leaders of intergovernmental and nongovernmental organizations, scholars, members of the intelligentsia?

Given the general orientation of the New Haven approach, it would seem that they seek to find authority not just in expectations of decision-making elites of states, but in a broader group of elites.[58] Anthony D'Amato argues that the New Haven scholars, "seem to view 'authoritative' so broadly as to encompass just about any decision made by an international decisionmaker."[59] I believe, especially given the desires of the New Haven scholars for inclusivity, that they would examine an even larger group of elites than Professor D'Amato suggests, not just "international decisionmakers." As such, the group whose perceptions of authority are used in assessing law is much larger than the group sought by positivists in determining *opinio juris*.

In light of this larger group, how does a New Haven scholar "measure" authority and control? What does he or she examine to determine the existence of authority and control and, therefore, law?

In an essay entitled "The Identification and Appraisal of Diverse Systems of Public Order,"[60] McDougal and Lasswell preliminarily spell out the process of gathering information on the nature of a public order system. In the process, scholars would of necessity determine expectations of authority and control. This process is described briefly in a section called "What the Scholar Does in Gathering and Processing Data." In a nutshell, they prescribe three "operations" in which the scholar should engage to get the appropriate information. In "Operation 1," the researcher is to "establish the provisional identity of a public order system within a community context by means of an inventory of explicit legal formulae."[61] What this means in the international context is that the scholar should examine treaties, resolutions, and other formal indices of authority and control. It is important to note, however, that with respect to authority, these formal items are not dispositive. As McDougal, Lasswell, and Reisman explain elsewhere, "there can . . . be no automatic assumption of identity between formal and actual controlling institutional structures and expectations of authority."[62] Operation 2 moves the scholar a bit further. In that undertaking, the scholar is urged to "add accuracy and detail to the inventory obtained by *Operation 1* by describing the frequency with which each prescription found in the legal formulae is invoked or purportedly applied in controversies."[63] In other words, the scholar will examine how often the formal expressions of authority are really controlling. Finally, Operation 3 calls on the scholar to "analyze all other sources for the purpose of making a fuller identification of the systems of public order provisionally revealed by the preceding operations.[64] The scholar should "describe the legal process in the context of the decision process as a whole, and of the social process within the entire community."[65] "Most of the scholarly effort at this phase," they explain, "is devoted to obtaining data by methods that are not conventional to traditionally trained legal scholars."[66]

The procedure they have in mind can be reinforced by examining some comments that McDougal, Lasswell, and Reisman make in another article that discusses authority. "Genuine expectations of authority," they explain, "are discerned by contextual examination of past decision as well as by the utilization of all the techniques of the social sciences for assessing the current subjectivities of individuals."[67] Hence, McDougal and colleagues seem to suggest that the scholar needs to do two additional things. First, he or she needs to examine the responses of individuals to various cases in which a normative question arises ("contextual examination of past decision"). For example, to determine whether it were legal for a state to engage in forcible intervention abroad to rescue its nationals, a scholar would examine how "members of the community" responded when such intervention took place. What were their perceptions of the legitimacy (i.e., the authority) of such intervention? Second, McDougal and company suggest that other social science methods ("all the techniques of the social sciences") should be used to assess perceptions of authority. These techniques could, presumably, run the gamut from content analysis of official documents to actual surveying and interviewing the "members of the community."

If this is the case, then the third question logically follows. We can measure authority and control using recognized methods, but how much authority and control is necessary for something to be called "law"? What threshold must be achieved for "law" to exist? Like the traditional positivists, the New Haven scholars are well aware of the difficulty of finding this threshold. Moreover, they seem to suggest that the amount of these two elements necessary for law will vary depending upon the case. For example, McDougal, Lasswell, and Reisman note that "the precise degree of effectiveness or 'control' required for 'law'—whether in national or international arenas—cannot . . . be stated absolutely; it is a function of context and will vary."[68] Professor Moore seems to reflect this contextual approach when he notes that "whether or not one postulates any particular combination of authority and control as the most useful definition of law for a particular purpose, the observer of the legal system must be concerned with patterns of authority and patterns of control."[69] In "The Identification and Appraisal of Diverse Systems of Public Order," McDougal and Lasswell note, almost in passing, that "as a matter of definition it will often be clarifying for the scholar to specify the minimum level of frequency of invocation and purported application that he requires before accepting a particular pattern of authority and control as 'law.'"[70] In essence, the New Haven School avoids setting any standard authority-control threshold; it will vary from case to case, and perhaps even from scholar to scholar.

From the preceding analysis, the New Haven method for determining the existence of international law would appear to be reasonably clear. If the scholar identifies the expectations of authority in conjunction with a certain amount of control, there is law. But much of the New Haven literature suggests that there are other factors that the scholar may use in the determination of law. In "Some Basic Theoretical Concepts about International Law: A Policy Oriented Framework," Professor McDougal explains that "international law" is "the process of authoritative decision *insofar as it approximates a public order of human dignity*."[71] Here the author is suggesting that law is not purely authority and control, but rather authority and control if they promote the goal of "human dignity." In effect, the New Haven scholars seem to assume that there is an international community[72] that has the promotion of human dignity as its highest goal. Accordingly, legal scholars are to find the law in the authoritative and controlling decisions that promote that goal. As Professor Friedrich Kratochwil notes, this signals a "teleological orientation to law."[73] Kratochwil explains that "law in this conception is no longer susceptible to a clear statement in rules or precedents, but consists in an agglomeration of shifting and interacting standards, policies, and preferences of the various decision-makers."[74] As a consequence, "the legal character of a decision has to be ascertained by means of an appraisal which includes the description of past trends, factors affecting the decision, projection of future trends, and evaluations of policy alternatives in terms of the overarching goal of human dignity."[75] Under this logic, therefore, an international legal rule exists not merely when there is a sufficient degree of authority and control, but only when the putative rule is directed toward the promotion of human dignity. This idea that is present in some of the New Haven literature greatly complicates the more straightforward authority-control approach.

A Critique of the New Haven Approach

Almost since the New Haven approach was developed, other scholars have provided many extensive critiques. The purpose here is not to dissect what Kratochwil has called "McDougal's exceedingly complex 'theory' *about* law."[76] Instead, this section will attempt to provide a basic critique of the primary elements of the New Haven method for determining law.[77]

One of the most useful contributions of the New Haven approach is the introduction of the concepts of authority and control. These two concepts, as will be discussed below, can serve as excellent tools for ascertaining both the objective and subjective element of international law. But there are a number of difficulties with these concepts as the New Haven scholars develop them.

First, as noted above, McDougal and associates seem to seek expectations of authority not only in the decision-making elites of states, but also in a much larger group, the members of the international community. This raises many problems. How does a scholar determine who belongs to this group? Ideally, the New Haven scholars submit, it is to consist of all individuals in the world. But at present, it is the "effective elite." Who are these people? Moreover, the claim that the expectations of authority of individuals of this broader group should be sought seems to reject a fundamental proposition in the current international system: states make the law. It is thus the expectations of the decision-making elites in *states* that should be sought. Perhaps at some future point the international system will become so differentiated that other actors will play an unmediated role in the law-creating process, but that is not yet the case.

Second, as has been noted above, McDougal and company view authority as expectations concerning the method through which a decision was produced. This clearly reflects these scholars' understanding of law not as a body of rules but as a process. Yet, if one does regard law as a body of rules, a body of rules produced through a process, but a body of rules nonetheless, that scholar is going to be most concerned about whether a putative legal rule is perceived to be law *now*—irrespective of whether the process was legitimate. While ideally, as observed above, a rule that is produced through a legitimate method would itself be perceived to be legitimate, this is not always the case. As a consequence, I believe that the authoritativeness of the *rule* is still the indicator of the subjective element of a rule of international law.

Third, the contradictory ways in which the New Haven scholars define law presents not only logical difficulties but also proposes a definition of law that clearly is not law. If law were the conjunction of authority and control alone, scholars would have a reasonably clear criterion. But, as noted above, the New Haven scholars also suggest that law may be authority and control insofar as they promote human dignity. There are many problems here. What is human dignity? At one point, McDougal and Lasswell define human dignity. "The essential meaning of human dignity as we understand it can be succinctly stated,"[78] they say. Human dignity, they continue, "refers to a social process in which values are widely and not narrowly shared, and in which private choice, rather than coercion, is emphasized as the predominate modality of power."[79] But what does this mean? And why postulate human dignity as the "overarching goal"? McDougal and colleagues seem to recognize that there is no absolute philosophical necessity in positing human dignity as the goal of the international community, but seem to do so because it is, so they allege, recognized universally. "All systems," they contend, "proclaim the dignity of the human individual and the ideal of a worldwide public order in which this ideal is authoritatively pursued and effectively approximated."[80] Do all systems truly accept human dignity as a goal? Is it possible to reach any kind of international consensus on the meaning of this term? Does "human dignity" mean the same to decision-making elites in the United States as it does to those in Iran, China, or Nigeria?

The New Haven School's focus on human dignity—while commendable from a moral perspective—introduces into the law-determining process an extremely subjective element. As Professor Kratochwil notes, this aspect of the New Haven method reintroduces a "natural law" conception.[81] Kratochwil argues that "even if we agree that human dignity is of overarching importance, it is rather questionable whether such a teleological conception of human actions can provide us with standards sufficiently precise to come to a consensus as to what is to count as law."[82] Moreover, I do not believe we can agree. In the diverse international system, there is, at present, no one conception of human dignity that the decision-making elites have affirmed.

A PROPOSED METHODOLOGY

In light of the preceding examination of traditional positivism and the New Haven approach, this section will set forth the basic contours of a new method for determining rules of international law. This method will draw on the insights of both positivism and the New Haven School while attempting to avoid the pitfalls of these approaches. Accordingly, this section will do two things. First, it will lay out the fundamental assumptions that animate this proposal. Second, it will explain the essence of the proposal itself.

Fundamental Assumptions

Throughout the course of this book, I have expressed several basic assumptions about the nature of the international system in general and the international legal system in particular. At risk of repetition, I would like to note these assumptions here. It is, I believe, extremely important to make very clear the foundation upon which this methodology is constructed. First, I assume that the international system is an "anarchic" system. This, of course, means that the system is anarchic in the formal sense.[83] There is no centralized legislative, executive, or judicial body. The system is not anarchic in the literal sense of the word; it is not completely without governance or law. Second, I assume that states are the primary actors in the international system. While I recognize a plethora of nonstate actors—and indeed an ever-increasing role for these actors—states remain the major players. Third, I assume that states are essentially unitary actors. Notwithstanding the complicated internal workings within states, I believe that for purposes of understanding international legal rules and their creation, states can be discussed as unitary actors. Fourth, I assume that in this decentralized international system, states are sovereign. While there is a great deal of debate within the academic community about the precise meaning of "sovereignty," the term is employed as noted in the previous chapter. Sovereignty means that all states are juridically equal; accordingly, they can be bound by law only through their consent. In the absence of a law to which states have consented, they are therefore legally allowed to do as they choose. Fifth, I assume that states consent to the creation of international law in three basic ways: treaties, custom, and general principles. "General principles" I take to mean the two consent-based definitions provided earlier: general principles of law found in the domestic legal systems of states and general principles about the nature of the international legal system.

The Proposed Methodology

The Basic Authority-Control Test

In light of these assumptions about the international system and international legal rules, the best test for determining the existence of a rule of international law is what might be called the "authority-control" test.[84] Drawing on the language developed by the New Haven School, a putative rule of international law can be regarded as "law" if it possesses authority and control. First, the decision-making elites in states must perceive the rule to be authoritative; they must perceive it to be law. There must be *opinio juris*. Second, the rule must be controlling. It must be reflected in the actual practice of states.

This approach uses the language and basic concepts of the New Haven School, but there are three important differences. First, as noted above, the New Haven approach uses perceptions of the "members of the international community" to determine the existence of authority. I believe this phrase is too vague to put into practice. Moreover, at present, international law is created by states. As a consequence, it is the decision-making elites in states that participate in the law-creating process. Accordingly, it is the perceptions of these individuals—those involved in the day-to-day policy making and policy implementation of states—whose perceptions of authority matter. Second, the concept of authority in New Haven parlance relates to perceptions that the process by which the "decision" is rendered is authoritative. As explained earlier, I believe that the critical subjective element is whether the putative *rule* itself is seen to be the law—not whether the process is perceived to be legitimate. Accordingly, in keeping with a basic assumption of positivism, I will use the concept of authority to describe the authoritativeness of the rule. In other words, authority, as employed here, is a synomyn for *opinio juris*. Third, the New Haven scholars suggest that there can also be a teleological element to the determination of a rule of law. International law becomes something that is authoritative and controlling insofar as it promotes human dignity. While I personally believe that human dignity should be a goal of the international system, I do not believe that it should be used in the process of determining *legal* as distinct from *moral* rules. Law is created by states. If they choose to enshrine human dignity in legal rules, that is commendable. But the task of the legal scholar must not be to impose his or her definition of morality onto the legal system, but rather to identify those rules that states have in fact created.[85] Indeed, as discussed in chapter 1, it is only in refusing to conflate morality with legality that the moral deficiencies of the law can be identified.

How does this approach work in practice? Under the authority-control test, if a scholar or decision maker is called on to determine the existence of a rule of international law, he or she would ask two questions: Is it authoritative? And is it controlling? Irrespective of the particular source of international law—custom, treaty, or general principle—the same fundamental test can be applied.

The application of this approach to putative rules of customary international law is fairly clear. Asking if a rule is authoritative and controlling is essentially the same as asking if there is *opinio juris* and if there is state practice. If, for example, someone were to suggest that it was a rule of customary international law that public warships passing each other on the high seas must display a particular light configuration, the investigation would be very straightforward. First, a scholar would engage in the empirical examination. He or she would observe such vessels passing and determine if they did, in practice, display the appropriate light configuration. Second, the scholar would then determine if the decision-making elites in states believe that this practice is required by law—if they believe that this practice is authoritative. If the scholar determined that there was a practice and that the practice was, in fact, perceived by these elites to be authoritative, then it could be concluded that there was a rule of customary international law requiring that naval vessels display this particular light configuration when passing each other.

Applying this approach to international conventions, may seem a bit more difficult. Traditional positivists would claim that in most circumstances the very existence of a treaty would indicate that there was a rule of international law.[86] But, as noted earlier, if a treaty or a particular provision of a treaty is neither authoritative nor controlling, states no longer consent to that rule. One way to view this is to argue that under the doctrine of *rebus sic stantibus* the treaty or provision is no longer law because there has been a fundamental change of circumstances. If states no longer believe the rule is authoritative and if it is not controlling, there seems to have been a very fundamental change in circumstances. Some scholars, however, might object to this argument. Under the Vienna Convention on the Law of Treaties, they would argue, there is a formal procedure for invoking the doctrine of "fundamental change of circumstances." Unless this formal procedure is followed, the treaty is still the "law."[87] If, however, one were to argue that *rebus sic stantibus* is regarded as a general principle about the nature of international law, it would lie at the very heart of the consent process. A fundamental a priori assumption of states, it could be contended, is that they are not bound by treaty provisions if a fundamental change occurs. Accordingly, notwithstanding the formal requirements in the Vienna Convention, if a treaty is lacking in authority and control, it is not law. But a scholar need not take recourse to the controversial doctrine of *rebus sic stantibus*.[88]

A second—and more appropriate—way to approach the application of the authority-control test to treaties would be to make the following argument. When a treaty is concluded and enters into force, there is a *presumption* that authority and control exist. In formulating and ratifying the agreement, states are expressing a belief in the authoritativeness of the treaty and pledging to carry out the provisions of the treaty in their practice. If, however, as time passes, the treaty as a whole, or a particular provision of the treaty, loses authority and control, the putative rule contained in the treaty or the provision no longer reflects the willingness of states to restrict their behavior in a given way. Once states are no longer willing to restrict their behavior, as sovereigns, they are legally free to do as they choose. If, for example, a treaty provided that all states were required to guarantee to their citizens paid vacations, once that treaty entered into force, it would create the presumption that there was a legal obligation to grant paid holidays. But if most states did not grant such holidays and statements of decision-making elites and other manifestations indicated that there were low perceptions of authority with respect to the putative rule, it would seem that states were no longer willing to be bound by this restriction, and, accordingly, it would no longer be considered a *legal* rule.

It should, of course, be noted that in making this argument, I am not suggesting that a *single* violation or even *several* violations by states are in and of themselves sufficient to remove the legal obligation contained in a treaty provision. For example, when Iranian authorities consented to the holding of American diplomats hostage in 1979, that act constituted a violation of the Vienna Convention on Diplomatic Relations. The Iranian action *did not* alter the provision of the Convention dealing with diplomatic immunity. The Iranian act was illegal. Only if there were substantial indication that a treaty provision generally lacked authority and was generally not controlling of behavior, could one conclude that the provision was no longer law.

In short, it seems clear that treaties are susceptible to the authority-control test. In order for consent to remain the basis for the creation of international law, states must be able to alter treaty provisions through new authoritative practice. As a consequence, while a treaty creates a presumption of the existence of a legal rule, unless that treaty or the provision in question is still authoritative and controlling, it is not the law. States have effectively withdrawn their consent.

Finally, this test could also be applied to general principles of law. For general principles of law found in the domestic legal systems of states, a scholar would undertake this two-prong test. If, for example, estoppel is submitted to be a general principle in this sense, the scholar would first attempt to determine if the principle were controlling. Do the municipal legal systems in the world use estoppel in domestic cases? Then, the scholar would ask if these legal systems regard this principle as authoritative—do they perceive it to be law. If estoppel is found to have both these qualities, it can be said to be a rule of law.

Measuring Authority and Control

While the general nature of the authority-control test can be set out in a fairly straightforward fashion, a more difficult question is how to measure authority and control. In other words, what elements would a scholar consult to be able to determine if a putative rule possessed authority and control? Over the years, legal scholars have suggested a wide variety of methods for determining the necessary components of a rule of international law. What follows is one attempt to opera-tionalize the authority-control test. Clearly, this is not the only way of fleshing out the authority-control test. But it is, I hope, a useful method.

Authority.   A putative rule is authoritative when the decision-making elites in states perceive the rule to be authoritative. What in-dicators can a scholar use to determine if this perception exists? There are, no doubt, a variety of factors that would help an observer deter-mine the extent to which a putative rule is perceived to be authorita-tive. A rough indication of the authoritativeness of a rule can be gained from asking the following questions.

1. **Are there manifestations of authority? And if so, how many?** Here the scholar is asking if there are clear representations that the decision-making elites in states perceive the putative rule to be authori-tative. In asking this question, the scholar should look for both *formal* and *informal* manifestations of authority. Examples of such formal manifestations would include treaties, United Nations Security Council resolutions, domestic laws, executive orders, and domestic judicial decisions. These kinds of items all have a certain solemnity that would reflect an official indication that a particular rule is perceived to be authoritative.

This type of manifestation can be illustrated in operation in the following example. Suppose, for instance, one submitted that it were a rule of international law that diplomats should not be arrested. A scholar might first look at existing treaties[89]—both bilateral and multi-lateral. Are there provisions in these treaties that prohibit the arrest-ing of diplomats? If there are, that would indicate certain perceptions of authority. Are there Security Council resolutions that affirm the inviolability of diplomats? During the Gulf War, for example, the Security Council adopted numerous resolutions upholding various principles of international law. Even though these dealt with a very specific case, the resolutions represented nonetheless formal reaffirmation of the principles involved.

But while it is convenient to have formal manifestations of authority, often they are not present. This does not necessarily mean that perceptions of authority are low. There may be other indicators of authority, including public statements by leaders and spokespersons for states, speeches in parliaments, negotiating documents, diplomatic notes, letters or memoranda. A scholar should consult these indicators of authority as well as the more formal manifestations.

2. How universal are the manifestations of authority?
Virtually all scholars would agree that in order for a rule of general international law to exist—one that is globally valid—there has to be nearly universal acceptance of the authoritative nature of the rule. In other words, the greater the number of states that accept the rule as authoritative, the higher the overall authoritativeness of the rule. This acceptance can be identified by finding positive manifestations coming from a particular state or by noting acquiescence on the part of a state when other states assert the authoritativeness of the rule. While it is certainly possible that a rule of international law can exist on a less-than-universal basis,[90] for a rule to be proclaimed general international law, there must be exceptionally "wide-spread"[91] perceptions of authority.

In addition, as the International Court of Justice noted in the *North Sea Continental Shelf* cases, for there to be a rule of customary international law, there must be the participation of those "states whose interests are specially affected."[92] In the case in question, the Court was discussing the procedure for the delimitation of the continental shelves for states that are adjacent. As a consequence, the states "whose interests are specially affected" would be those in similar situations—in this case, those adjacent states with continental shelves. What the Court was saying was that it would be impossible for a rule of customary international law relating to the delimitation of continental shelves to develop, unless those states that had a direct stake in the rule had participated. In a broader context, this principle suggests that for any global rule of international law to exist, the participation or acquiescence of certain states—those whose interests are specially affected—is virtually mandatory. It would thus follow logically that in any assessment of authority, special weight should be given to the views of these states. An example may serve to illustrate. Let us suppose some states claim it is a rule of international law that states launching spacecraft had to file copies of the flight plan with the Secretary General of the United Nations. If 188 states have expressed strong indications that the rule is authoritative, but the United States and Russia—traditionally two of the major actors in space travel—do not believe that the putative rule is required by law, the authority accorded to that would-be rule is exceedingly low.

3. How significant are the manifestations of authority?

Not only is it critical that there be many manifestations of authority coming from nearly all members of the international community, these manifestations of authority most also be *significant*.[93] If a lower-level State Department official sends a cable claiming that a particular behavior reflects the law, that is a manifestation of authority. But if the president of the United States issues an Executive Order contending that this behavior is the law, that is a more significant manifestation of authority. Needless to say, the more significant the manifestations of authority, the greater the overall authority of the putative legal rule.

Another factor that affects significance relates to the frequency of both formal and informal manifestations of authority. The more frequent the manifestations, the easier it is to conclude that the putative rule is authoritative. If, for example, states issue memoranda on a monthly basis that support a particular rule relating to transit passage, an observer would be more secure in pronouncing the rule to be authoritative than a case where such memoranda came infrequently. Accordingly, the scholar should factor in frequency when making judgments about the significance of the manifestations.

4. Are there contrary manifestations of authority?

A final question that can be used to examine the authority of a particular rule relates to what might be called "contrary manifestations" of authority. It is possible that there may be many indications that a particular rule is authoritative and, at the same time, various manifestations that a rule is not authoritative. For example, there may be numerous formal and other manifestations of authority supporting the existence of a rule prohibiting the use of force to collect contract debts of nationals abroad.[94] But even as states are proclaiming the authoritativeness of this rule, they may be sending other signals that it is permissible to use force for this purpose. Hence, there may be treaties and presidential statements declaring that it is illegal to use force to resolve these debts *and* memoranda and other presidential speeches that express a belief that is it permissible to use force to recover contract debts. If this were the case, these contrary examples would detract, and perhaps cancel out, the positive examples of authority. Because states frequently send mixed signals of this kind, it is important that the scholar be certain to look for such contrary manifestations of authority.

Control. In order for a would-be legal rule to be a genuine rule of international law, it must have authority *and* control. Not only must the decision-making elites perceive the rule to be law, but also the rule must be reflected in state practice. The rule must be controlling of state behavior. But how can a scholar measure control? What indicators exist to enable an observer to determine if a rule is, in fact, reflected in practice? As with authority, I believe that there are several questions that a scholar or practitioner can ask that will provide a rough indication of the control enjoyed by a putative legal rule.

1. **Are there violations of the rule? If so, how many?**
The most basic question that the scholar should ask relates to violations of the putative rule. If there are frequent and widespread violations of a particular "rule," it is very difficult to conclude that the rule is truly controlling of state behavior. If a rule purports to prohibit the arresting of diplomats, but an examination of state practice indicates that diplomats are frequently arrested, the rule is not really controlling. Conversely, if there are no violations of a particular rule, then the rule is controlling; it is reflected in practice.

2. **How universal are the violations of the rule?**
If one state violates a particular rule with great frequency, the rule may still have a large degree of control provided the violations are not widespread throughout the international community. The scholar must, therefore, inquire about the universality of violations. How many different states in the international system violate the rule? And, most important, the scholar must ask if the states "whose interests are specially affected" by the rule comply. If these states do not follow the rule, this behavior would indicate that the control of that rule was very low.

3. How serious are the violations of the rule?

A final criterion that can be used to evaluate the control of a would-be rule is the seriousness of the violation.[95] If one U.S. marine stationed at Guantanamo Base shoots, without being provoked, at Cuban nationals walking outside the base, that is a violation of a rule of law. But this single action should not count the same as a concerted action by the entire contingent of American forces at the base to attack civilians outside the base.

Indexing Authority and Control

While there are undoubtedly many different ways to approach these questions about authority and control, I believe that these issues can be translated into a form that will provide a rough method of indexing authority and control. In other words, by assigning certain numerical values to a series of more specific questions, a rough number can be assigned to the authority and control of a particular rule. While there is nothing sacred or absolute about such quantification, it can provide a useful guide to the scholar who wishes to compare differing degrees of authority and control accorded different putative rules.

Clearly, it is always dangerous to attempt any kind of quantification of intangible things such as authority or control. Many subjectivities enter into the calculations. Nonetheless, in the field of international relations, efforts have been made to provide rough quantifications of other elements. Numerous scholars have, for example, attempted to provide indices of "power."[96] Such efforts allow scholars to compare the relative power of states, which allows them to better understand the role these states can play in the international system. Similarly, various individuals and groups have undertaken to provide indices of "freedom." The human rights organization Freedom House, for example, prepares a yearly survey in which states are categorized as "free," "partially free," or "not free."[97] Some scholars have even attempted to measure nonlegal "norms." Recently, for example, Professors Gary Goertz and Paul F. Diehl sought to measure the decolonization norm.[98] My attempt here is to follow in the spirit of these efforts—to provide the scholar with a plausible method of better assessing the authority and control of a putative rule. The index in the appendix to this chapter is one possible way of attempting to quantify authority and control. Other types of indices may be ultimately more useful. Indeed, I hope that one consequence of this suggested index will be to encourage others to devise indices that will serve as even better tools for assessing authority and control.

The proposed index is divided into two sections—one for authority and one for control. For each of those two elements, the scholar will pose a series of specific questions that seek to address the more general questions about authority and control that were discussed above. Each question has a scale from 0 to 5 points that correspond to different answers. So, for example, a scholar may ask how many manifestations of authority exist with respect to a particular putative rule. If there are "many" such manifestations, the scholar will award a particular number of points; if there are "several" manifestations, the scholar will award less points; if there are "few" manifestations, the scholar will give even less points. And if there are no formal manifestations, the scholar will award no points. While it is clearly a subjective determination on the part of the scholar, or other observer, as to what words such as "many," "several," or "few" mean, this approach provides more consistency than traditional approaches.

With numerical values assigned to both the authority and control of a particular rule, the two factors can be plotted on a simple x–y graph as depicted below.

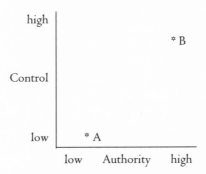

This depiction allows the observer to note the degree to which a particular rule is perceived to be authoritative and the degree to which it is controlling. As a consequence, it enables the scholar to make judgments about whether the would-be rule is law.

But how much authority and control are necessary for a putative rule to be considered a *legal* rule? Here there is no simple answer. It is clear that rules that enjoy both a very high degree of authority and control would be considered law (point B). The rule that states can have no more than a twelve-nautical-mile territorial sea would fall into this category. The decision-making elites in probably all states would claim that this rule is law and their flagships would behave accordingly. Hence, this rule and other rules that enjoy this level of authority and control would clearly be law. At the other end of the continuum are putative rules that enjoy little authority and little control (point A). An example might be a putative rule that every person has a right to holidays with pay.[99] While this provision is contained in the Universal Declaration of Human Rights, it lacks authority. Most government officials in the world would probably claim this to be an aspiration, not a legal right. Moreover, the provision is not truly reflected in the practice of states. A large percentage of the world's population are not guaranteed paid holidays by the state.

The question of the legal status of the rules becomes more complicated when dealing with rules located elsewhere on the graph. What about a rule at point Y, where there is a high degree of control, but a low degree of authority? Or, conversely, what about a rule at point Z, where there is a high degree of authority, but a low degree of control? Or, finally, what is the legal status of a rule at point X, where there is a moderate degree of both authority and control?

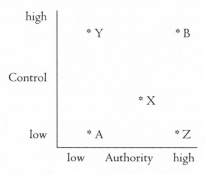

For putative rules at points X, Y, and Z, it is impossible to set an absolute standard against which the legal status of the rule could be judged. As a consequence, there will likely be disagreements among scholars and decision-making elites about putative rules in these ranges. This should not be a reason to despair. Even in domestic legal systems, there are areas where different courts and other authoritative decision makers have very different assessments about what the law is. In a sense, this problem reflects the essence of the law-creating process. Law is dynamic. Hence, at any point in time, some putative rules may be in this middle range—somewhere between being clearly law and being clearly not law. Nonetheless, there is a substantial body of rules that have both a high degree of authority and a high measure of control. This proposed index will, it is hoped, assist the scholar in identifying these rules.

CONCLUSION

This methodology set out in this chapter offers, I believe, several advantages. First, it is firmly based on the notion that international legal rules are created through the consent of states. The authority-control test allows the investigator to gage both the degree to which states have accepted the legitimacy of the putative rule and have put it into practice. As such, the test avoids the teleological element present in the New Haven approach. Second, the methodology provides a guide that scholars and others can use to provide a rough numerical valuation of authority and control. At present, scholars have no explicit way of weighing authority and control. Accordingly, scholarly analysis reflects a scholar's "feeling" that a particular rule has a certain amount of authority or control. While the index presented here is no magical formula and is fraught with subjective choices, it allows for some formal guide. In particular, it permits a single scholar to evaluate a variety of rules using essentially the same criteria. Moreover, the index can assist a wide range of decision makers by providing one—albeit not the definitive—assessment of state practice. If, for example, a legal advisor to a foreign ministry is attempting to determine if it is illegal to use force to rescue nationals, indexing that rule would provide one useful bit of information that could figure into the overall assessment. It would provide a systematic way to evaluate the putative legal rule. And to the extent that such an index helps systematize the method for examining state practice, it can make an important contribution to jurisprudence.

APPENDIX: A PROPOSED INDEX FOR ASSESSING AUTHORITY AND CONTROL

Authority Index

I. Manifestations of Authority

A. Number of manifestations
How many manifestations of authority are there?

o	1	2	3	4	5

| None | Few | Several | | Many |

B. Universality of manifestations
How universal are the manifestations of authority?

o	1	2	3	4	5

| No states[a] | Few states[b] | Several states | Most states | All states |

C. Significance of manifestations
How significant are the manifestations of authority?

o	1	2	3	4	5

| Not significant | Not very | Somewhat | Fairly | Most significant |

II. Contrary Manifestations of Authority

A. Number of manifestations
How many contrary manifestations of authority are there?

o	−1	−2	−3	−4	−5

| None | Few | Several | | Many |

[a] *OR*, any number of states but *without* all or most of those states whose interests are specially affected.

[b] *OR*, any number of states, but *without* a *few* of those states whose interests are specially affected.

B. Universality of manifestations
How universal are the contrary manifestations of authority?

o	−1	−2	−3	−4	−5
No states	Few states	Several states	Most states[c]	All states[d]	

C. Significance of manifestations
How significant are the contrary manifestations of authority?

o	−1	−2	−3	−4	−5
Not significant	Not very significant	Somewhat significant	Fairly significant	Most significant	

Maximum Authority Points   15
Minimum Authority Points   0[e]

Control Index

I. Number of Violations of the Putative Legal Rule
How many violations of the putative rule occur?

o	1	2	3	4	5
Many		Several		Few	None

[c]*OR*, any number of states, but *without* a *few* of those states whose interests are specially affected.

[d]*OR*, any number of states but *without* all or most of those states whose interests are specially affected.

[e]If the "contrary manifestations of authority" are more numerous, more prevalent, and more significant than the "positive" manifestations of authority, the results would technically produce a negative number. If this is the case, it is clear that the rule is not authoritative in any meaningful sense. As a consequence, for purposes of tabulating authority and plotting it on a graph, a net negative score on the Authority Index would still be plotted as "o." To take a bizarre analogy, if a person fails an examination with a grade of 56%, he or she receives an "F" for failure. If another student earns a grade of 30%, he or she still receives an "F" for failure. An "F-" makes little sense. Thus, if the net result of the Authority calculation is -4, it will still be tabulated as "o."

II. **Universality of Violations of the Putative Legal Rule**
How universal are the violations of the putative rule?

0	1	2	3	4	5
All states[f]	Most states[g]	Several states	Few states	No states	

III. **Seriousness of Violations of the Putative Legal Rule**
How serious are the violations of the putative rule?

0	1	2	3	4	5
Most serious	Fairly serious	Somewhat serious	Not very serious	Not serious	

Maximum Control Points   15
Minimum Control Points   0[e]

THE INDEX ILLUSTRATED

In order to understand the way in which the index can be used, this next section will provide an illustration. First, the illustration will explore how the index could be applied to determine the existence of a rule of general international law—that is, a rule of customary international law that is globally valid.[100] Second, the illustration will discuss how the index could be applied to determine the existence of a rule of conventional international law.

A Rule of General International Law

We begin by selecting the putative rule that is to be tested. Because it is assumed that states can behave as they choose, unless there is a specific rule prohibiting that behavior, the rule must be phrased as a prohibitory rule. We will select the putative rule that it is illegal for a host state to arrest diplomatic personnel from another state. For purposes of this example, the question we are asking is this: Is it a rule of general international law that a host state cannot arrest diplomatic per-

---

[f]OR, any number of states but *with* violations by all or most of those states whose interests are specially affected.

[g]OR, any number of states, but *with* violations by a *few* of those states whose interests are specially affected.

sonnel from another state. With this rule selected, we can now begin asking questions based on the index. Since this is an illustration, I will be assuming certain facts rather than conducting the full empirical investigation that an actual application of the index requires.

AUTHORITY INDEX

Section I asks if there are manifestations of authority. Question I(A) calls for the examination of the "Number" of these manifestations. Here we examine both formal and other manifestations of authority. Clearly, there are numerous formal manifestations—the Vienna Convention is the most notable. But there are also a variety of domestic laws that prohibit the arresting of diplomats. In the United States, for example, the Diplomatic Relations Act prohibits arresting such persons.[101] Most other states have followed suit. There are also other manifestations of authority, such as numerous presidential statements, memoranda, and other less formal indicators upholding this principle. Thus, for "Number" we will award a "5."

Under I(B), it is clear that these manifestations come from all states in the system. Thus, under "Universality" we will award a "5" for all states. Since all states essentially have an equal stake in questions related to diplomatic immunity, there are no "states specially affected." Accordingly, questions relating to that category do not figure into this particular calculation.

Finally, under I (C), it also seems clear that the manifestations of authority are "Most Significant." They come from treaties and other sources indicating the highest level of state support. We will thus award a "5" in this category as well.

Section II asks if there are contrary manifestations of authority. Clearly, there are no treaties, domestic laws, or other such indications. The closest thing to a contrary manifestation came from Iran during the Hostage Crisis of 1979–1981, when that state seemed to claim that its actions were permissible due to past American violations of Iran's sovereignty. But that is an extremely isolated incident. Accordingly, "–1" is awarded for II (A) "Number."

Under II(B), "Universality," since this contrary manifestation really came from only one state, I would award it "–1" as well.

Finally, under II(C), "Significance of manifestations," given that Iran was the single noncompliant state that made this claim, I would consider Iran's action "Not Very Significant," and award "–1."

This calculation yields a total score of "12" on the Authority Index. Given that "15" is the maximum score, "12" would indicate a very high level of authority. Now, the Control Index can be calculated.

CONTROL INDEX

Section I asks about the number of violations of the rule. It is impossible to conclude that there are no violations, especially given the Iranian Crisis and other scattered actions against diplomats, such as those that committed by Iraq during the Gulf War. But given the thousands of diplomats and the relatively few arrests, we will award "4" points for these very few violations.

Section II then asks about the universality of violations. Again, there are a few states that have violated the rule. Accordingly, we will give a "4" in this category. Since, as noted above, there are no states with special interests, those issues do not figure into this example.

Finally, Section III asks about the "Seriousness of the Violations." Certainly, incidents such as the Iranian Hostage Crisis and Iraqi actions during the Gulf War are quite serious. But these are isolated incidents. As a consequence, when the seriousness over time is assessed, I would rate it "3"—for "Somewhat Serious."

Given this calculation, the control index is at "11." This is almost as high a score as the authority index. Plotting the two indices on a graph, yields the following result:

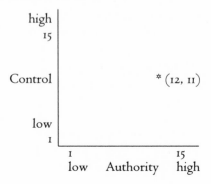

With both a high degree of authority and a high degree of control, the rule prohibiting the arrest of diplomatic personnel can be considered a rule of general international law.

A Rule of Conventional Law

In the above example, we assumed that we were attempting to determine if the rule in question were a rule of general international law. As a consequence, conventions, such as the Vienna Convention on Diplomatic Relations, would be examined as one—albeit a very significant—indicator of authority. But what if the question that we were exploring was whether the rule in question is valid as a matter of treaty law? As noted earlier, I believe that the same basic authority-control test can be applied to treaty law as well as to a rule of customary international law. The difference is that when a treaty has been concluded on a particular matter, there is a *presumption* that the treaty is authoritative and controlling. In the context of this index, the mere existence of the treaty would reflect a most significant manifestation of authority. Accordingly, under section I of the Authority Index, an investigator would award a "5" under each category—Number of manifestations, Universality of manifestations, and Significance of manifestations. This would yield the maximum authority points, "15." But then the investigator would be required to explore any "Contrary Manifestations." Despite the existence of a treaty, it is possible that states would be claiming that it was permissible to act contrary to the treaty. If there were such contrary indications, this would be subtracted from the 15 points awarded due to the existence of the treaty. It is thus possible that there may be a treaty on a particular matter, but many widespread and significant contrary manifestations of authority so as to cancel out much or all of the authoritative effect of the treaty. In applying the Control Index for treaties, one would proceed in the same manner as with a rule of general international law.

NOTES

1. Prosper Weil, Towards Relative Normativity in International Law?, 77 *Am. J. Int'l L.* 413, 415 (1983).

2. Id. at 433.

3. See Georg Schwarzenberger, *The Inductive Approach to International Law* 9–13 (1965).

4. Speaking of natural law writers in general, Professor Schwarzenberger observes that their treatises contained "quotations from the Bible, Church fathers, classical writers, mythology, history, and State practice."Id. at 11.

5. Id. at 13.

6. Schwarzenberger speaks of the "raw material of international law." George Schwarzenberger, *The Inductive Approach to International Law*, at 33.

7. Id. at 5. Professors McDougal, Lasswell and Reisman explain that positivism, or what they call "analyticalism," "focuses principally upon the strict application of a variety of rules emanating from fixed authoritative sources and holds that the appropriate function of jurisprudence, even at its loftiest levels is the syntactic clarification of the interrelations of such rules." Myres S. McDougal, Harold D. Lasswell & W. Michael Reisman, Theories About International Law: Prologue to a Configurative Jurisprudence, reprinted in Myres S. McDougal & W. Michael Reisman, *International Law Essays* 43, 92 (1981).

8. McDougal, Lasswell & Reisman, Theories About International Law, at 92.

9. Hans Kelsen, *Principles of International Law* 305 (1952).

10. Id. at 342.

11. It is interesting to note that in the 1969 Vienna Convention on the Law of Treaties, the term *rebus sic stantibus* is not used. Instead, that convention refers only to a "fundamental change of circumstances." Vienna Convention on the Law of Treaties, art. 62.

12. Hans Kelsen, *Principles of International Law*, at 359.

13. Id.

14. Id. at 360.

15. Id.

16. Prosper Weil, Towards Relative Normativity?, at 430.

17. Id. at 425.

18. Id. at 427.

19. Id.

20. Id. at 417.

21. Id.

22. See his comments in 1 Hersch Lauterpacht, *Collected Papers* 56–58 (1970), where he expresses his reservations about positivism.

23. Id. at 61.

24. Hans Kelsen, *Principles of International Law*, at 307. Kelsen, of course, recognizes that "the frequency of conduct, the fact that certain actions or

abstentions have repeatedly been performed during a certain period of time, is only one element of the law-creating fact called custom." Id. *Opinio juris* is the "second element." Id.

25. 1 Hersch Lauterpacht, *Collected Papers*, at 61.

26. Id.

27. Hans Kelsen, *Principles of International Law*, at 304.

28. Id. at 305–307.

29. Id. at 395.

30. Id. at 394.

31. Id.

32. Id.

33. H. C. Gutteridge, 21 *British Yearbook of International Law* 5 (1944), cited in Georg Schwarzenberger, *The Inductive Approach to International Law*, at 36–37.

34. U.N. Charter, art. 2, para. 4 (1945).

35. This is the thesis of Anthony Clark Arend & Robert J. Beck, *International Law and the Use of Force: Beyond the U.N. Charter Paradigm* (1993).

36. This is the claim made by Professor Edward Gordon, for example. Gordon explains that

> the rule embodied in Article 2(4) is not just a freestanding rule of customary law; it is also a formal treaty obligation. States may withdraw their consent to be bound by treaty obligations, but may not simply walk away from them.

Edward Gordon, Article 2(4) in Historical Context, 10 *Yale J. Int'l L.* 271, 275 (1985). Gordon argues: "The existence of an operational code [which I take to mean 'state practice'] different from the formal commitment may be cause for withdrawing state consent, but it does not supplant the process for withdrawing consent called for by the treaty or by treaty law generally." Id.

37. See Graham C. Lilly, Law Schools without Lawyers? Winds of Change in Legal Education, 81 *Va. L. Rev.* 1451 (1995) ("The 'policy-science' of Myres McDougal and Harold Lasswell, once in the limelight, is now a distant memory.").

38. This is a point often made by Professor William V. O'Brien.

39. Myres S. McDougal & Harold D. Lasswell, The Identification and Appraisal of Diverse Systems of Public Order, reprinted in *International Law Essays*, at 15, 20.

40. Id. at 20.

41. Id.

42. Id.

43. Id.

44. Id. at 21–22.

45. Id. at 22.

46. Id.

47. John Norton Moore, Prolegomenon to the Jurisprudence of Myres McDougal and Harold Lasswell, 54 *Va. L. Rev.* 662, 666 (1968).

48. Id.

49. John Norton Moore makes a similar argument.

50. Myres S. McDougal & Harold D. Lasswell, The Identification and Appraisal of Diverse Systems of Public Order, at 22.

51. Id.

52. Myres S. McDougal, Harold D. Lasswell & W. Michael Reisman, The World Constitutive Process of Authoritative Decision, reprinted in *International Law Essays*, at 191, 192.

53. Id.

54. Id. (footnote omitted).

55. Myres S. McDougal, Harold D. Lasswell & W. Michael Reisman, Theories About International Law, at 56.

56. Myres S. McDougal, Harold D. Lasswell & W. Michael Reisman, The World Constitutive Process of Authoritative Decision, reprinted in *International Law Essays*, at 191 (emphasis added).

57. Id.

58. This argument has been made elsewhere. Anthony Clark Arend & Robert J. Beck, *International Law and the Use of Force*, at 206–207.

59. Anthony D'Amato, *International Law: Process and Prospect* 11–12 (1987).

60. Myres S. McDougal & Harold D. Lasswell, The Identification and Appraisal of Diverse Systems of Public Order, at 38.

61. Id.

62. Myres S. McDougal, Harold D. Lasswell & W. Michael Reisman, The World Constitutive Process of Authoritative Decision, at 191.

63. Myers S. McDougal & Harold D. Lasswell, The Identification and Appraisal of Diverse Systems of Public Order, at 39.

64. Id.

65. Id.

66. Id.

67. Myres S. McDougal, Harold D. Lasswell & W. Michael Reisman, The World Constitutive Process of Authoritative Decision, at 191 Id.

68. Id. at 192.

69. John Norton Moore, Prolegomenon to the Jurisprudence, at 666.

70. Myres S. McDougal & Harold D. Lasswell, The Identification and Appraisal of Diverse Systems of Public Order, at 39.

71. Myres S. McDougal, Some Basic Theoretical Concepts about International Law: A Policy Oriented Framework, in 2 Richard A. Falk & Saul Mendlovitz, eds., *The Strategy of World Order: International Law* 129 (1966) (emphasis added).

72. Professor Trimble notes this aspect of the New Haven approach. Phillip R. Trimble, International Law, World Order, and Critical Legal Studies, 42 *Stan. L. Rev.* 811, 815–818 (1990).

73. Friedrich V. Kratochwil, *Rules, Norms, and Decisions* 195 (1989).

74. Id.

75. Id.

76. Id. at 196–197.

77. This section draws upon the critiques of the New Haven School found in Friedrich V. Kratochwil *Rules, Norms, and Decisions*, at 193–200, and Phillip R. Trimble, International Law, World Order, and Critical Legal Studies.

78. Myres S. McDougal & Harold D. Lasswell, The Identification and Appraisal of Diverse Systems of Public Order, at 24.

79. Id.

80. Id. at 19.

81. Friedrich V. Kratochwil, *Rules, Norms, and Decisions*, at 197.

82. Id.

83. See Robert J. Lieber, *No Common Power* (3d ed. 1995).

84. This approach has been applied in some of our previous work. See Anthony Clark Arend & Robert J. Beck, *International Law and the Use of Force*, at 9–10; Anthony Clark Arend, International Law and the Recourse to Force, 27 *Stan. J. Int'l L.* 1 (1990).

85. In the *South West Africa* case, the International Court of Justice made the same point:

> Throughout this case it has been suggested, directly and indirectly, that humanitarian considerations are sufficient in themselves to generate legal rights and obligations, and that the Court can and should proceed accordingly. The Court does not think so. It is a court of law, and can take account of moral principles only in so far as these are given sufficient expression in legal form.

South West Africa Case, 1966 I.C.J. 6, 34. See also Anthony A. D'Amato, *The Concept of Custom in International Law* 77 (1971) for a discussion of this point.

86. Interestingly enough, Hans Morgenthau raises this criticism of positivism. Hans Morgenthau, Positivism, Functionalism, and International Law, 34 *Am. J. Int'l L.* 260–84 (1940). I am indebted to Professor Robert J. Beck for pointing out Morgenthau's argument.

87. I am grateful to Professor Don Piper of the University of Maryland who presented this critique of this argument.

88. Previously, I have made the argument that *rebus sic stantibus* is such a general principle of international law. After reflection, I am less inclined to believe this. Even though scholars such as Hedley Bull have argued in favor of this concept as a constitutive principle of the international legal system, the efforts by the international community in recent years to greatly limit the application of this doctrine indicate that it probably does not have this status. Michael Akehurst, for example, has noted the degree to which this doctrine was previously regarded. He explains that "in previous centuries writers tried to explain this rule by saying that every treaty contained an implied term that it should remain in force only as long as circumstances remained the same (*rebus sic stantibus*) as at the time of conclusion." Michael Akehurst, *A Modern Introduction to International Law* 140 (6th ed. 1992). But, Akehurst continues, "such an explanation must be rejected, because it is based on a fiction, and because it exaggerates the scope of the rule." Id. "In modern times," Akehurst explains, "it is agreed that the rule applies only in the most exceptional circumstances; otherwise it could be used as an excuse to evade all sorts of inconvenient treaty obligations." Id.

89. In this case, it should be noted, treaties are being used as *one indicator* of authority. This is similar to the way in which treaties were cited by the United States Supreme Court in the *Paqueta Habana* case. In that case, the Court was attempting to determine the legal rule dealing with the seizure of fishing vessels that was binding on the United States and Spain. Since there was no bilateral or multilateral treaty on this issue to which Spain and the United States were parties, the Court had to establish if there were a rule of customary international law. In an effort to make that determination, one thing the Court cited were various other bilateral and multilateral treaties in an effort to evince practice. Similarly, I am suggesting that treaties can be used as examples of formal manifestations of authority in the determination of a rule of general international law. If a scholar is trying to determine the law for a particular state or groups of states, a treaty to which those states are party is, as noted earlier, a prima facie indicator of the rule between those states. Nonetheless, the authority and control of that rule should also be tested as explained above.

90. The International Court of Justice upheld the concept of less-than-universal international law in the *Asylum* case. *Asylum Case* (Columbia v. Peru), 1950 I.C.J. 266.

91. In the *North Sea Continental Shelf* cases, the International Court of Justice refers to the need for "widespread" *practice*. *North Sea Continental Shelf Cases* (Fed. Rep. Ger. v. Den.) (Fed. Rep. Ger. v. Neth.), 1969 I.C.J. 3, at para. 73.

92. *North Sea Continental Shelf Cases*, 1969 I.C.J. 3, at para. 74.

93. I am most grateful to an anonymous reviewer for bringing this factor to my attention. I draw here upon his or her comments on a earlier draft of this book.

94. I was inspired by Professor Martha Finnemore to use this example.

95. This factor was also raised by an anonymous reviewer of an earlier draft of this work.

96. See, e.g., Ray S. Cline, *World Power Assessment 1977: A Calculus of Strategic Drift* (1977).

97. See, for example, R. Bruce McColm, et al., eds., *Freedom in the World: Political Rights & Civil Liberties 1990–1991* (1991) as an example of this approach.

98. Gary Goertz and Paul F. Diehl, Toward a Theory of International Norms: Some Conceptual and Measurement Issues, 36 *J. Conflict Res.* 634–664 (1992).

99. I am indebted to Dr. David Little of the U.S. Institute of Peace for noting this issue.

100. This same approach, as indicated in the text above, would apply to general principles of law common to domestic legal systems. The only significant difference is that the investigator would be looking at the authority and control in the domestic setting.

101. Diplomatic Relations Act, 22 U.S.C.A. sec. 254a–e.

FOUR

LEGAL RULES AND INTERNATIONAL POLITICS

As noted in the introduction to this book, one question that has occupied recent scholarship of international relations theorists has been the role that norms and institutions play in contemporary international politics. A great debate has ensued between structural realists and institutionalists of various varieties about whether normative concerns need to be considered in order to understand behavior in the international system. Do "rules," "norms," and "institutions" really "matter"? Or are normative questions essentially irrelevant to an accurate assessment of the world of international politics? Are norms merely epiphenomenal? Unfortunately, in much of this scholarly debate, there has been little explicit discussion of the role *legal* rules play in international behavior. This chapter seeks to focus specifically on that issue. What role do legal rules play in international politics? Even if an acceptable methodology for determining the existence of legal rules can be developed—as the previous chapter has attempted—do legal rules matter in international relations? Do they affect international politics in a significant way?[1]

It is an essential premise of this chapter that how an individual assesses the role of legal rules depends upon one's framework for under-

III

standing international relations at the broadest level. In other words, the theory of international relations to which a scholar or practitioner subscribes will influence, if not determine, his or her perception of the relationship of legal rules to politics. Accordingly, this chapter will explore several prominent contemporary approaches to international relations and examine how these approaches could address the role of legal rules. While some of these approaches are not extremely explicit in how they address international *legal* rules, I will attempt to take the major assumptions of each approach and apply that logic to an examination of legal rules. The first section will discuss structural realism—the approach that has dominated thinking about international relations for nearly the last two decades. The second section will then examine what has been called "rationalist institutionalism." This approach challenges many of the assumptions and conclusions of structural realism, arguing that rules can play a role in international politics. The third section will explore what is perhaps the most recent challenge to structural realism—constructivism. Constructivism, I will argue, provides the most useful approach for understanding contemporary international relations. Drawing upon this argument, the fourth section will use constructivism to present several propositions about the role of international legal rules in international politics.

STRUCTURAL REALISM

Structural Realist Theory

Following World War II, "realism" became the most widely accepted approach for understanding international relations. Tracing its roots to Thucydides,[2] classical realism was articulated by such notable thinkers as Hans Morgenthau, George Kennan, E. H. Carr, and Reinhold Niebuhr. In many respects, much of the writings of classical realists exhibit a desire to expose the fallacies of the so-called idealist approach of the earlier part of the twentieth century. According to some of these realists, idealism, with its optimistic assumptions about the goodness of humanity and the potential for international law and international institutions, prevented statespersons from acting in conformity with the "realities" of the international system. Indeed, many realists would argue that it was these false assumptions about politics that helped lead to the tragedy of World War II.[3]

While the various advocates of classical realism differ in the specifics of their approaches, there were certain core assumptions of the realist model.[4] Realism recognizes the duality of human nature: people are both good and evil. As a consequence, human beings are not perfect, nor are they perfectible.[5] This assumption about human nature translates into a conception of international relations in which neither states nor the international system as a whole is perfect or perfectible. Instead, the international system is a competitive environment where states struggle with each other to survive. Accordingly, a prudent statesperson seeks to pursue national survival by obtaining power. For it is only in the garnering of power that a state can preserve itself against the conflicting goals of other states. Order can obtain in such a system in the balancing of interests that results as states pursue power.[6]

Structural realism[7] draws upon the basic assumptions of classical realism, but develops a more thorough and extremely parsimonious theory for understanding international relations. Kenneth Waltz is probably the most noted structural realist, with his 1979 book *Theory of International Politics* serving as the classic articulation of the theory. A number of other prominent scholars such as Robert Gilpin, Joseph Grieco, Robert J. Lieber, and John Mearsheimer also fall into the structural realist camp. Although many works have been written by structural realists that state the fundamental assumptions of this approach, one of the most recent examinations comes from Professor Mearsheimer. In an article entitled "The False Promise of International Institutions," Mearsheimer sets forth five basic assumptions that structural realists make about the international system. Other structural realists may provide a different list of assumptions, but Mearsheimer's five assumptions capture, I believe, the essence of structural realism and can provide the basis for our understanding of this approach.[8]

First, Mearsheimer asserts that structural realists believe "that the international system is anarchic."[9] "Anarchy," he explains, "is an ordering principle, which says that the system comprises independent political units (states) that have no central authority above them."[10]

The international system is not an anarchy in the common usage of the word—utter chaos and complete conflict[11]—but rather it is a "formal anarchy"[12] because there is "no common power."[13] As Mearsheimer puts it, "there is no higher ruling body in the international system."[14] "There is," he explains, "no 'government over governments.' "[15]

Second, Mearsheimer explains that structural realists believe that "states inherently possess some offensive military capability, which gives them the wherewithal to hurt and possibly destroy each other."[16] In short, "states are potentially dangerous to each other."[17]

Third, given the reality of the second assumption, Mearsheimer argues that realists assert "that states can never be certain about the intentions of other states."[18] Since states have the potential to engage in offensive military operations against other states, it is always a possibility that any given state will use military force against any other state. A statesperson never knows what a state will do. He or she can never have absolute trust in another state.

Fourth, Mearsheimer claims that structural realists believe that "the most basic motive driving states is survival."[19] Here he echoes a fundamental tenet of classical realism. Indeed, it was Hans Morgenthau who referred to the "moral principle of national survival."[20] All statespersons seek to preserve the independence of their state.

Fifth, structural realists assume that "states think strategically about how to survive."[21] For Mearsheimer, "states are instrumentally rational."[22] They engage in rational calculations about the best steps that they can take to secure their survival in the international system.

Based on these five assumptions, Mearsheimer claims that states will engage in what he calls "three main patterns of behavior."[23] First, according to him, states will "fear each other."[24] Because each state has the potential to launch offensive military actions against each other—and perhaps the motivation—there will be mutual fear among states. This fear is exacerbated by the lack of a central authority to mediate conflicts and punish aggressors. As a consequence, "states have ample reasons to take steps to be prepared for war."[25] Second, following from this first point, Mearsheimer believes that "each state in the international system aims to guarantee its own survival."[26] Without any common mechanism to promote order, states will take a variety of measures on their own to survive. While these actions may involve the establishment of alliances, "alliances are only temporary marriages of convenience, where today's alliance partner might be tomorrow's enemy, and today's enemy might be tomorrow's alliance partner."[27] Finally, Mearsheimer asserts that "states in the international system aim to maximize their relative power position over other states."[28] What he means here is that states are not only concerned about their absolute power vis-à-vis other states, but also their relative power. If the United States has more power than Japan, for example, it will still be concerned about relative gains in Japanese power, even if the United States continues to have more power in an absolute sense. As Mearsheimer explains, "the greater the military advantage one state has over other states, the more secure it is."[29] While this contention has been disputed by some theorists,[30] it is certainly one plausible realist belief. Indeed, Waltz himself argues that "the first concern of states is not to maximize power but to maintain their position in the system."[31]

To summarize Mearsheimer's argument, structural realists believe that the international system lacks a common power and is thus anarchic. As a consequence, states are extremely insecure. A state can never be certain that one of its fellow states will not use military force against it. Accordingly, states must engage in "self-help" measures to attempt to survive in the international system. They do this by attempting to enhance their power within the system. It thus follows from these assumptions that if a scholar wishes to understand international behavior, he or she must understand the underlying power distribution in the international system.

Structural Realism and International Legal Rules

In light of this picture of international relations, what place do legal rules have in structural realism? How does law influence the behavior of states? The classical realists wrote a great deal about international law. Hans Morgenthau, himself trained as an international lawyer, even chose to devote a chapter in his classic *Politics Among Nations* to "The Main Problems of International Law."[32] Similarly, George Kennan is well known for his critique of what he called the "legalistic-moralistic approach" in American foreign policy.[33] Few structural realists, however, have explicitly applied their approach to international law.[34] In fact, in Waltz's *Theory of International Politics* there is no discussion of international legal rules as such. But even though most structural realists have not explored the role of legal rules in depth, many of them have addressed normative concerns more generally. They have explored the roles of "regimes," "rules," "norms," and "institutions" in international politics. The logic of their arguments on these normative issues can, I believe, easily be translated to international legal rules per se.

Following from their understanding of the nature of international relations, the structural realists have generally denied any real independent force to "rules," "norms," and "institutions." Since states are engaged in the pursuit of power to secure themselves in the international system, normative considerations are merely convenient tools for states. "Regimes" or other normative arrangements come about when they serve the power interests of states. When these arrangements no longer serve those interests, they are abandoned. As Professor Susan Strange has observed, "all those international arrangements dignified by the label regime are only too easily upset when either the balance of bargaining power or the perception of national interest (or both together) change among those states who negotiate them."[35] Hence, "regimes" cannot be regarded as independent variables in international relations. Professor Krasner summarizes this structural realist position quite clearly. "Regimes," he notes, "if they can be said to exist at all, have little or no impact."[36] "They are," he continues "merely epiphenomenal."[37] What really affects the behavior of states are underlying political and economic factors.[38] For the structural realist, "regimes are excluded completely, or their impact on outcomes and related behavior is regarded as trivial."[39] Or to put it another way, structuralist "orientations are resistant to the contention that principles, norms, rules, and decision-making procedures have a significant impact on outcomes and behavior."[40]

In view of this rather dismissive approach to normative constraints generally, it seems that the structural realist would not place a great deal of hope in legal rules in particular. A realist conception of the international system would see states concluding treaties and formulating customary international legal rules as suited their immediate interests. In fact, under the realist paradigm, the specific legal rules that were created would generally reflect the interests of the most dominant states. As Professor Robert Gilpin has argued, "although the rights and rules governing interstate behavior are to varying degrees based on consensus and mutual interest, the primary foundation of rights and rules is in the power interests of the dominant groups or states in a social system."[41] And, since the legal rules were developed to serve state interests, states would not really feel constrained from violating these rules if they believed that violation would be in their interest. To the structural realists, therefore, legal rules would be epiphenomenal. If they affected the behavior of international actors at all, it would only be at the margins.[42]

A Critique of Structural Realism

As a theory of international relations, structural realism has much to its credit. The recognition of the anarchical nature of the international system and the role of states as primary actors seem quite consistent with reality and reflect assumptions that underlie the writings of most international legal scholars. Moreover, structural realism is fairly parsimonious. It has, especially during the cold war, demonstrated a great deal of explanatory power.[43] Nonetheless, reams of paper have been spent criticizing various aspects of structural realism.[44] It clearly lies beyond the purpose of this book to engage in a lengthy critique of the entire edifice of structural realism. A few comments, however, can be offered about the structural realist approach to normative concerns and its implications for international law.

First, structural realism assumes that the anarchical nature of the international system will inevitably lead to insecurity and thus competition for power. But, as scholars such as Alexander Wendt have argued, anarchy in and of itself does not necessarily lead to this competitive striving for power. As Wendt notes, "anarchy is not a structural cause of anything."[45] He explains that "what matters is its social structure, which varies across anarchies."[46] "An anarchy of friends," Wendt argues, "differs from one of enemies, one of self-help from one of collective security, and these are all constituted by structures of shared knowledge."[47] In other words, states in different settings will respond to the anarchical situation differently. Depending upon the attitudes shared by the decision-making elites in states, states could respond to the anarchical condition through the creation of legal rules that will provide the background for cooperation and the mitigation of conflict. Or they could respond by establishing a competitive self-help system in which legal rules are merely conveniences.

Second, and more fundamentally, structural realism assumes that the identity and interests of states are exogenously determined.[48] As used in this book, the identity of a state—or any other international actor for that matter—is how it conceives of itself and its role in the international system. This identity, of course, will vary in different contexts. In the military arena, for example, the United States may have the identity of a nuclear superpower. In the realm of international trade, the United States may have a completely different identity. Interests, as employed here, are the specific foreign policy goals of international actors that flow from their identity.

What the structural realists argue is that states enter the international playing field with established identities and interests that flow from these identities.[49] They then engage in rational calculations to improve their power position in the international system. Legal rules come and go to suit this goal. But what if participation in an international legal regime actually alters the identities and interests of states?[50] Structural realism does not really take into account the possibility that states can become *different in nature* through their participation in the international legal system. A structural realist asks if states find it in their interest to follow legal rules, rather than if legal rules change the interests, and indeed, the very identity, of states. If legal rules do have this effect, they clearly play a critical role in international behavior.

Finally, realism's failure to differentiate legal rules from other types of rules ignores the distinctiveness of legal rules. If the decision-making elites in states perceive legal rules to be fundamentally different from other rules, the effect legal rules produce in international relations may be different from the effect of other "norms," "rules," and "institutions." By lumping all varieties of "rules" together, the structural realists may have missed an important factor in international politics for the sake of parsimony.

RATIONALIST INSTITUTIONALISM

Rationalist Institutionalist Theory

For a number of years now, other international relations scholars have attempted to provide an alternative vision of international politics. In particular, these scholars have sought to provide a theory of international relations that assigns a much greater role to international "institutions" and other normative considerations. In a classic article published in 1988,[51] Professor Robert Keohane sought to distinguish two different approaches to institutions that he believed existed within the discipline of political science. The first he called the "rationalist institutionalist" approach. The second he called the "reflective" approach. After a number of years, this distinction still appears useful in understanding two broad ways in which scholars view the relationship of normative concerns. Using this distinction, this section will explore the rationalist approach to international institutions.[52] It will set forth the fundamental assumptions of the approach and then attempt to apply the logic of the approach to legal rules. The next section will explore what Keohane called the "reflective" approach—what is being called here "constructivism."

Generally speaking, the rationalist institutionalists share many of the same assumptions about the international system as do the structural realists.[53] They believe that states are the primary actors in the international system, that states behave essentially as unitary actors, and that the international system is anarchic. Rationalist institutionalists also assume that states behave as rational actors, seeking to maximize their interests.[54] They submit, however, unlike most structural realists, that the creation of "institutions" and "regimes" can serve the interests of states and can even have some independent influence on state behavior. In making this assertion, the rationalists draw a great deal upon economics and economic theory to assess the benefits to be gained through this form of cooperation.

In order to better understand the rationalist institutionalist approach to normative considerations, it is necessary to explore two important concepts that have dominated much of this literature: institutions and regimes. Both these terms are used in a variety of ways by different scholars. Indeed, in some cases, the two terms seem almost to mean the same thing. While an exhaustive survey of the various definitions would be nearly impossible, a few representative definitions should be sufficient to illustrate the nature of these concepts.

In most international *legal* scholarship, the word "institution" refers to a formal organization such as the United Nations, the International Sea-Bed Authority, or the Organization for Security and Cooperation in Europe.[55] In the international relations literature, however, the term frequently has a broader meaning. Professor Keohane, for example, defines institutions as "persistent and connected sets of rules (formal and informal) that prescribe behavioral roles, constrain activity, and shape expectations."[56] Under this definition, an institution could be a formal international organization, but it could also be a much more informal arrangement. Professor Oran Young, in an even broader definition, contends that "international institutions are social institutions governing the activities of members of the international community."[57] Social institutions for Young "are identifiable practices consisting of recognized roles linked by clusters of rules or conventions governing relations among the occupants of these roles."[58]

Similarly, the word "regime" has also been used in a variety of different ways.[59] One of the earliest uses came from Dean John Gerard Ruggie. In 1975, Ruggie defined a regime as "a set of mutual expectations, rules and regulations, plans, organizational energies and financial commitments, which have been accepted by a group of states."[60] Several years later, Professor Krasner concluded that regimes are "sets of implicit or explicit principles, norms, rules, and decision-making procedures around which actors' expectations converge in a given area of international relations."[61] In a similar vein, Professor Oran Young submitted that "regimes are social institutions governing the actions of those involved in specifiable activities or sets of activities."[62] "Like all social institutions," he explains, "they are practices consisting of recognized roles linked together by clusters of rules or conventions governing relations among the occupants of these roles."[63] Thus, for Young, what differentiates an international institution from an international regime is its specificity. A regime deals with a very specific activity or group of activities, while an institution deals with international activity more broadly.

— rationalist thy to do → create regime/just.

Irrespective of which definition of regime or institution one chooses, the point of the rationalists is that states do, in fact, create institutions and regimes. And these institutions and regimes can play significant roles in the behavior of international actors. In the cost-benefit calculations of states, the rationalists argue, it makes sense to cooperate— at least at times—through the creation of a regime. And over time states may follow the rules of the regime, even though they may conflict with their immediate self-interest. Why is this the case?

good idea to coop, at times, thru regime

Throughout the rationalist literature many advantages to participation in institutional arrangements have been discussed. I will note several here. First, institutions reduce transaction costs.[64] By cooperating with other states, states can pool resources, share information, and reduce transaction time. Such benefits will encourage states to create regimes and discourage unilateralism.

why participate in institutions

Second, regimes may stabilize expectations.[65] In order for any state to realize its goals in the international system, a high degree of predictability of the behavior of other states is optimal. As a consequence, states could find it in their interests to create institutional arrangements that regulate state behavior. Even though the states entering such arrangements may be sacrificing some autonomy, they calculate to gain in the long run by being able to anticipate how other states will behave.

lose a little, gain more

Third, regimes may lengthen the "shadow of the future"[66] and thereby promote cooperation. If a state knows that it will interact with another state only once, the shadow of the future is nonexistent. Thus, the state can pursue its short-term goals without regard to the need to interact with the other state on subsequent occasions. Institutional arrangements, however, provide for repeated interactions among states and thus lengthen the shadow of the future. If a state knows that it will be engaging in many transactions over time through such an institutional arrangement, it will need to be concerned about its long-term relationships with other states.

increase interactions shadow of future

Fourth, institutions may also provide for decentralized enforcement of regime rules through the creation of situations of reciprocity.[67] The following example may serve to illustrate. Let us assume that a regime regarding the admission of foreign nationals is established. Under the rules of the regime, all states will grant resident status to nationals of other regime parties. If, contrary to the rules, France decided not to

for deco dist — decentralized enforcement

grant such status to Sierra Leonean nationals, Sierra Leone could reciprocate and refuse to grant resident status to French nationals. This reciprocal connection may induce all parties to comply with the rules of the regime.

But even while the rationalists identify these and other benefits to be accrued from participation in international institutions, rationalist scholars argue that the interests of states remain paramount. Despite the advantages of participation in a regime, if a state believes that its interests are no longer served by a regime, it will act contrary to the rules of the regime. Indeed, many scholars of this orientation would argue that in certain areas, such as security, regimes are unlikely to be established.[68] These scholars tend to believe that economic and resource areas are the most likely candidates for effective regimes. In these areas, they would argue, cooperative behavior is likely to be more beneficial than unilateral actions.[69]

Professor Krasner has graphically depicted this approach to regimes. In "Structural Causes and Regime Consequences: Regimes as Intervening Variables," he presented the following figure:[70]

$$\text{Basic causal variables} \xrightarrow{\text{b}} \text{Regimes} \xrightarrow{\text{b}} \text{Related behavior and outcomes}$$
$$\searrow \quad \text{a} \quad \nearrow$$

Krasner explains that "for most situations there is a direct link between the basic causal variables [the underlying political and economic goals that motivate states] and related behavior (path a); but under certain circumstances that are not purely conflictual, where individual decision making leads to suboptimal outcomes, regimes may be significant (path b)."[71] In other words, when an issue strikes at the core security concerns of a state, political and economic factors will more likely be the sole determinant of state behavior. Only in areas outside this core do regimes really seem to affect behavior.

Rationalist Institutionalism and
International Legal Rules

How would this approach apply specifically to legal rules? As with the structural realists, most of the rationalist institutionalists say very little about legal rules as such. But the logic of their approach can certainly be translated to "legal" regimes. In particular, what rationalist theory would suggest is that in areas of what might be called "low politics,"[72] legal rules would have a strong impact on state behavior. Issues of low politics would be those that do not strike at the core security concerns of states. Such issues would include certain trade and economic matters, international communication and transit, and some resource issues. In many of these areas, the benefits of cooperation would outweigh the benefits of unilateral action. Legal rules and legal regimes would provide the kinds of advantages that were discussed previously. They would, for example, reduce transaction costs and increase predictability of behavior. As a consequence, states would have great incentives to follow the legal rules in those areas. Accordingly, states will be likely to comply with rules relating to navigation, air transport, telecommunications, and the like. Thus, a rationalist institutionalist could conclude that the effect of legal rules on state behavior in these areas could be significant.

On the other hand, rationalists would probably argue that legal rules are not very significant in the areas of "high politics"—issues that *do* strike at the core security concerns of the state. In these areas, the factors that have the direct influence on state behavior would be the underlying political and economic goals—what Krasner calls the "basic causal variables." If the legal rules happen to coincide with these underlying goals, states will appear to be acting in accordance with the rules.[73] If, however, the legal rules conflict with other policy goals, states will almost certainly act contrary to the legal rules. Take for example, the invasion of Grenada by the United States in 1983. Even though an argument that an invasion of Grenada would violate international law was circulated among some U.S. officials, the United States did not perceive itself to be constrained—presumably because its vital interests were deemed to be at stake.[74]

A Critique of Rationalist Institutionalism

As with structural realism, the rationalist institutionalist approach offers many theoretical advantages. It seeks to grapple with norms and institutions and reintroduce normative conversations into international relations theory. Indeed, by refining the regime concept, the rationalists have been able to avoid the stigma that realists had attached to explicit references to "law" and "morality." Nonetheless, there has also been much criticism of the rationalist approach—both from within the structural realist camp and from outside of realism. In my brief discussion here, I wish merely to highlight some of the concerns about rationalist institutionalism as they touch directly on the question of legal rules.

First, in many respects, rationalist institutionalism does not go much beyond structural realism in its appreciation of the role of legal rules. The rationalists talk more about legal rules per se, but the distinctiveness of legal rules does not really figure prominently in their literature. But even beyond that concern, if the regime approach is applied to legal rules, the rationalists seem to be suggesting that legal rules only matter in certain areas of international politics. As noted earlier, the rationalists generally believe that regimes are most effective in areas relating to economic and resource issues, but not as effective in the security field. This argument when applied to law suggests that legal rules do not really "matter" in areas relating to the use of force or other security concerns. Viewed from a cynical perspective, one might be inclined to conclude that the rationalists are essentially saying that international legal rules do not really matter in the most important areas of international politics. In any case, the rationalists do not really provide any new insights on the role of legal rules in these areas.

Second, rationalist theory—like structural realism—does not explore the role legal rules can play in altering the identities and interests of states. Rationalists, too, seem to assume that state identities and interests are "exogenously given"[75] and do not really account for changes in identity caused by participation in international interactions, in particular, interactions in a legal regime.[76] This, in my opinion, ignores one of the most important contributions of legal rules to international politics, a contribution that is recognized in constructivism.

CONSTRUCTIVISM

While much of the debate among international relations scholars in the 1980s and 1990s has revolved around the relative merits of structural realism and rationalist instiutitionalism, a new approach to international relations theory began to emerge in the late 1980s. At the forefront of this new theoretical development have been scholars such as Professors John Gerard Ruggie, Friedrich Kratochwil, Nicholas Onuf, and Alexander Wendt. Over the course of its relatively short life in international relations scholarship, this approach has been called by several different names. As noted earlier, in 1988 Professor Keohane referred to it by the term "reflectivism."[77] Dean Ruggie now calls the approach "social constructivism." Following most of the recent scholarship in this area, I will use the term "constructivism."[78]

Where constructivism is situated in the larger international relations literature is a matter of some debate. It has many similiarities to the British "international society" approach,[79] which includes such writers as Hedley Bull, Martin Wight, and Adam Watson. The British approach "holds that the system of states is embedded in a society of states, which includes sets of values, rules, and institutions that are commonly accepted by states and which make it possible for the system of states to function."[80] This assumption is similar to that held by many contemporary constructivists.

Some scholars, such as Alexander Wendt, have contended that constructivism is a species of critical theory. From his perspective, critical theory is really a "family" of approaches to international relations.[81] Within this family are many different members. As Wendt notes, there are postmodern thinkers, such as Richard Ashley. There are neo-Marxists, such as Robert Cox. There are feminist writers such as Spike Peterson. And there are constructivists. According to Wendt, "what unites" critical theorists "is a concern with how world politics is 'socially constructed.'"[82] He explains that this "involves two basic claims: that the fundamental structures of international politics are social rather than strictly material (a claim that opposes materialism), and that these structures shape actors' identities and interests, rather than just their behavior (a claim that opposes rationalism)."[83]

In contradistinction to Wendt, Ted Hopf argues that "although constructivism shares many of the foundational elements of critical theory, it also resolves some issues by adopting defensible rules of thumb, or conventions, rather than following critical theory all the way up the postmodern critical path."[84] For Hopf, therefore, constructivism cannot truly be a form of critical theory because it is not fully post-modern. Yet, interestingly enough, Hopf goes on in his article to differentiate between "conventional" and "critical" constructivisms. It would thus seem that he is not really saying that "constructivism" is not a species of critical theory, but rather that a certain type of "constructivism" is not a type of critical theory.

In effect, Hopf's comment really makes a larger point: There are probably many varieties of constructivism itself. Indeed, according to Professor Ruggie, "there are sociological variants, feminist variants, jurisprudential approaches, genealogical approaches, an emancipatory constructivism and a more strictly interpretive kind."[85] All these approaches, Ruggie contends, seem to fall into three basic types. He calls these three types: neoclassical constructivism, postmodern constructivism, and naturalistic constructivism.[86] According to Ruggie, neoclassical constructivism is "rooted in the classical tradition of Durkheim and Weber."[87] For postmodern constructivism, Ruggie argues, "the intellectual roots are more likely to go back to Friedrich Nietzche and any updating to the writings of Michel Foucault and Jacques Derrida."[88] Naturalistic constructivism, Ruggie contends, "is grounded in the philosophical doctrine of scientific realism, particular the work of Roy Bhaskar."[89]

My purpose here is not to engage in a lengthy discussion of the varieties of constructivism, but rather to set forth what I believe to be the fundamental tenets of the constructivist approach to international relations and then apply that approach to international legal rules.[90] To do this, I will draw upon the insights of several scholars that fall into this approach, in particular Professors Wendt and Ruggie.

Constructivist Theory

Before exploring the fundamental differences between constructivism and other approaches to international relations, it should be noted that some, though not all, constructivists share with the structural realists many basic assumptions about the nature of the international system. Certain constructivists, like Wendt, believe that states are the primary actors in the system and that states behave essentially as unitary actors. They also believe that the structure of the international system is anarchic. And these constructivists believe that theorizing about the "system" is critical for an understanding of international relations.[91] Beyond these assumptions that some constructivists share with structural realists, however, constructivists part company with the structural realists. In particular, constructivists make two divergent assumptions about the nature of international politics.

First, constructivists assume that the structure of the international system is a "social structure." As Wendt notes, "neorealists think it [the structure] is made only of a distribution of material capabilities, whereas constructivists think it is also made of social relationships."[92] In other words, structural realists tend to believe that scholars can understand the structure of the system purely by measuring the "material resources"[93] of states—military might, economic resources, natural and physical resources, and the like. A structural realist would thus measure power by taking account of these kinds of material resources. How much military might does a state have? What is the size of its army? How many warships does it have? How sophisticated are its weapons systems? How great is its gross national product? Does it have important natural resources like oil or strategic minerals? But for constructivists, "social structures have three elements: shared knowledge, material resources, and practices."[94] As Wendt explains, "social structures are defined, in part, by shared understandings, expectations, or knowledge."[95] What exists "out there" depends to a degree upon how the decision-making elites in states commonly understand it. The mere existence of anarchy does not in and of itself lead to a competitive self-help system. It depends upon how states commonly understand that anarchy. The next element of "social structure" for Wendt is material resources. While constructivists recognize that things like "gold and tanks" exist, they "argue that material resources acquire meaning for human action through the structure of shared knowledge in which they are embedded."[96] As an example, Wendt notes that "500 British nuclear weapons are less threatening to the United States than 5 North Korean nuclear weapons, because the British are friends of the United States and the North Koreans are not, and amity or enmity is a function of shared understandings."[97] This seems to be essentially a reiteration of Wendt's first point. Reality depends to a large degree upon how states perceive the material conditions. Finally, "social structures exist, not in actors' heads nor in material capabilities, but in practices."[98] "Social structure," Wendt contends, "exists only in process."[99] What I believe he means here is that the social structure is not just what states "think" but rather how they behave based on what they think.[100]

In summary, constructivists contend that the international system is socially constructed, which means two things. First, there are certain concrete, material elements of the structure[101]—there are weapons, oceans, geographical conditions, people. These material elements, however, take on significance as states develop shared expectations through interaction. Thus, a relationship of enmity between two states exists not merely because those states have offensive weapons systems (material element), but because they harbor ill will toward each other (shared knowledge) and they engage in activities (practices) that reflect that attitude—weapons targeting, alliance formation, etc. Second, since constructivists argue that the international system is a social structure, they would recognize that certain "nonmaterial" elements also constitute part of the structure. In other words, they would acknowledge that states, through their practices, can generate certain norms of behavior (shared expectations). These norms would be just as much a part of the structure as the material elements.[102]

Second, while structural realists and rationalist institutionalists assume that the identity and interests of states are exogenously determined, constructivists believe that the interests and identities of states are created—at least in part—through interaction and can change through interaction. In an article aptly entitled "Anarchy Is What States Make of It: The Social Construction of Power Politics," Wendt explains that "actors acquire identities—relatively stable, role-specific understandings and expectations about self—by participation in . . . collective meanings."[103] "Identities," Wendt continues, "are the basis of interests."[104] Despite what other scholars might contend, "actors do not have a 'portfolio' of interests that they carry around independent of social context; instead, they define their interests in the process of defining situations."[105] What all this means is that there is, in effect, a mutually constitutive[106] relationship between structure and actor. States through their interactions help constitute the structure of the system, and the structure, in turn, shapes the identities and interests of states. This relationship means that participation in particular institutional arrangements can actually alter the very identity and interests of states. Describing this approach, Robert Keohane explains that "reflectivists" believe that "institutions do not merely reflect the preferences and power of the units constituting them: the institutions themselves shape those preferences and the power."[107] "Institutions," Keohane continues, " are therefore *constitutive* of actors as well as vice versa."[108] Consequently, "it is . . . not sufficient in this view to treat preferences of individuals as given exogenously: they are affected by institutional arrangements, by prevailing norms, and by historically contingent discourse among people seeking to pursue their purposes and solve their self-defined problems."[109]

Constructivism and International Legal Rules

Given these broad assumptions of constructivism, what insights can be gained from this approach with respect to the role played by legal rules in international politics? Here constructivism, like its relative, the British "international society" approach, has a great deal to contribute. Constructivist literature, like the British literature,[110] refers to international law much more than structural realists and rationalist institutionalists.[111] Most recently, Professor Andrew Hurrell, who describes himself as a "reflectivist," has written extensively about international law from this perspective.[112] Drawing upon this literature and the logic of constructivist theory, several conclusions can be made about what the theory implies for international law.

First, since constructivism asserts that the structure of the international system is a social structure, it would follow logically that international legal rules are part of the structure. State practice would evince a shared understanding that legal rules are a part of what makes up the international system. In other words, the structure "out there" would consist not merely of a group of self-regarding states with no common arbiter, but also a set of legal principles. In particular, there are two ways in which international legal rules form the structure of the international system: as "constitutive rules" and as "regulative rules."

"International law" as an institution itself[113] and certain specific international legal rules *constitute*, in part, the structure of the international system.[114] As Andrew Hurrell notes, "rationalist models miss the crucial link between the costs and benefits of specific legal rules and the role of international law as constitutive of the structure of the state system itself."[115] What does this mean? An oft given analogy is a game of chess.[116] The rules of chess are what Professor Kratochwil calls "constitutive rules."[117] They define what a game of chess is. While all individuals may wish to win the game, they cannot pretend that there are different rules. If they do, they are playing a game other than chess. In a similar fashion, Professor John Rawles notes the existence of "rules of a practice"[118]—his phrase for constitutive rules. He explains that "it is the mark of a practice that being taught how to engage in it involves being instructed in the rules that define it, and that appeal is made to those rules to correct the behavior of those engaged in it."[119] "Those engaged in a practice," Rawles notes, "recognize the rules as defining it."[120] Commenting on Rawles's point, Keohane notes: "Were the rules of a practice to change, so would the fundamental nature of the activity in question."[121]

Similarly, in addition to the "international legal regime" itself, there are certain specific constitutive legal rules of the international system. These legal rules help make up the international system as we know it. One scholar who has made this argument about the role of legal rules is Professor Stephen Kocs. For Kocs, there are certain "fundamental legal norms structuring the international realm."[122] These constitutive legal rules, argues Kocs, are not the great profusion of specific legal rules—a twelve-mile territorial sea, the inviolability of diplomats, the rules relating to extradition, or the like. Instead, the legal rules that structure the international system "exist . . . as a set of underlying, implicit rules which create a framework that allows formal agreements between states to be meaningful and binding."[123] These constitutive legal rules thus include first-order principles that provide the basis for the entire legal system—similar to what I have called "general principles about the nature of the international legal system." They may also include other rules that define the most fundamental relationships among the actors in the system.

What are these constitutive legal rules? In chapter 2, I list several candidates for first-order principles, such as the principle that international legal rules are created through consent and the principle of *do as you promise*

[*pacta sunt servanda.*] Professor Kocs cites Antonio Cassese's enumeration of eight constitutive legal principles. The first three, Kocs explains, "have existed as central features of the Westphalian legal order."[124] These are "the sovereign equality of states, nonintervention in the affairs of other states, and good faith [*pacta sunt servanda*]."[125] The next five principles, Kocs notes, "have emerged more recently."[126] These are "the self-determination of peoples, [the] prohibition on the threat or use of force, [the] peaceful settlement of disputes, respect for human rights, and international cooperation."[127] While I would dispute that some of these are truly constitutive legal principles,[128] Kocs's fundamental point about the existence of principles of this nature seems to clearly reflect the application of constructivism to legal rules.[129] In some sense, international legal rules constitute the international system.

The rest of the corpus of international law form "regulative rules,"[130] which are also part of the structure of the international system. These regulative rules *are* the vast array of specific international legal rules—the twelve-mile limit, the right of innocent passage, the prohibition on genocide, and so on—that students are taught in a basic international law class. Even though these rules do not constitute the system—in the sense of giving it foundational structure—they are still socially created and form part of the international system.

legal rules give foundational structure

Second, constructivists claim that there is a mutually constitutive relationship between "agent" and "structure." In particular, they claim that participation in a particular regime can alter the identity and interests of the actors. What all this means is that if states participate in a legal regime, the very act of participation can actually change how states see themselves and what they define as their particular interests. Structural realists would contend that states may create a particular legal regime because it supports their immediate interests.[131] When, however, their interests no longer coincide with the rigors of the legal regime, the realist would assert, states will not comply with the legal proscriptions of the legal regime. But a constructivist would assert that participation in the regime may have changed the identity and thus the interests of an actor. An example may serve to illustrate.

legal regime alters ident. + thus lasting regime

Under the United Nations Charter, states sought to establish a strict legal regime with respect to the use of force. As noted in the previous chapter, Article 2(4) prohibited the threat or use of force against the territorial integrity and political independence of states. The only two exceptions to this prohibition were force used in self-defense (Article 51) and force authorized by the Security Council (Article 41). During the cold war period, I would assert, states did not regard these provisions of the Charter to be authoritative, and they were not controlling of state behavior.[132] In the post-cold war period, however, it is possible that states will find the Charter arrangement to be in their interests. Initially, they may accept these legal rules as a short-term convenience. Over a longer period of time, however, state practice that reflects an acceptance of these rules may cause states to have a different sense of identity. They may see themselves as entities that "simply do not use force" against the territorial integrity or political independence of each other. The nonuse of force could thus become a major part of the identities of states. If this were to be the case, this practice would alter the specific interests (or goals) of states and, accordingly, their behavior. As states viewed themselves as "nonaggressors," their specific goals would not involve pursuits that necessitate the use of aggressive force.

A Critique of Constructivism

The constructivist approach to international politics has been subjected to much criticism in its relatively short life. In particular, international relations theorists have accused the constructivists of lacking empirical data for their conclusions.[133] How can one demonstrate that the structure of the international system is a "social structure"? And what evidence can be mustered to indicate that the identities and interests of states may change through participation in a particular regime? Yet despite these and other criticisms, the constructivist approach is particularly useful in the context of this book because it offers a great deal in its application to international legal rules. In many respects, it provides a theoretical framework for explaining what many international legal scholars take for granted. Most legal scholars probably take as a given the notion that certain fundamental legal principles help form the basis or, to use the constructivist term, *constitute*, the structure of the international system. But constructivism provides a more analytical way of understanding that phenomenon. In addition, constructivist thought presents an argument about how legal rules can become imbedded in the identities of states. While many international legal scholars would acknowledge that states create law to be in their interests, these scholars generally do not examine the way in which the goals of the legal principles and fidelity to those principles can become a part of state identity itself.

Despite these clear and significant contributions of constructivism, the theory is not above criticism. As noted earlier, a common criticism raised by the structural realists is the lack of empirical verification of constructivists' assertions. As research progresses, however, more and more empirical information is being provided. Professor Martha Finnemore, for example, has recently examined the role of the United Nations Educational, Scientific, and Cultural Organization (UNESCO) as a "teacher of norms." Her thesis is that through participation in UNESCO, states experienced changes in both their identity as states and specific interests.[134] Professor Finnemore has also engaged in an empirical study of humanitarian intervention.[135] In a similar fashion, other scholars have also begun to provide empirical support for constructivism.[136] Professor Audie Klotz, to take another example, has explored the development of international norms against apartheid.[137] It would thus seem that as time passes this supposed lack of data will become less of a criticism. As a consequence, I would raise two different concerns about constructivist theory as it relates to international legal rules.

First, given the mutually constitutive relationship between "agent" and "structure," it could be very difficult to determine exactly how one is affecting the other. Structural realism is easier. The actors' identities and interests are exogenously given. To understand how states will behave, a scholar need only look to the underlying power arrangements in the international system. But if the structure is changing the agent and vice-versa, how can a scholar accurately say anything about what is happening? A cynic might assert that constructivism presents a problem akin to determining where a circle begins and where it ends.

Second, since the structure for constructivists is a "social structure," the structure can only be understood in terms of "intersubjective meanings." In other words, through the process of interaction states gain a shared—hence "intersubjective"—understanding of the structure. But

given the multiple philosophical frameworks out of which the decision-making elites of states operate, can there really be intersubjective
meaning?[138] With respect to international legal rules, this problem
could be especially acute. As such scholars as Professor Adda Bozeman
have asserted, the very concept of "law" can mean very different things
to peoples in different cultures.[139] If this is the case, how can there be
a truly common perception of international law as part of the structure of the system?

The Arguments for Constructivism

While these concerns may present some difficulties for constructivism,
they are not insurmountable problems. In light of the nature of international relations, a very persuasive case can be made for the constructivist approach to international relations. First, I believe that the
structure of the international system is clearly a "social structure." In
the real world of international relations, individuals are the authoritative decision makers acting on behalf of states. As a consequence, it is
ultimately *individuals'* perceptions of the international structure that is
critical. Like Wendt, I believe that there are certain material "things
out there"—we cannot, for example, pretend that there is no ocean or
that nuclear weapons do not have deadly effects.[140] Nonetheless, how
this structure affects actors is largely contingent upon how they perceive that structure. As Wendt has observed, "the meaning of power
depends on the underlying structure of shared knowledge."[141] "A British build-up," he explains, "will be less threatening to the United States
than a North Korean one."[142] Perhaps the most significant example
of the socially constructed nature of the international system can be
seen in the end of the cold war.[143] As the Soviet Union under
Gorbachev was allowing radical change within Eastern Europe, that
state still possessed the same amount of nuclear weapons and other
instruments of war, yet it was clear that the cold war was over. The
Soviet Union was no longer the threat that it had been. Even though
much of the *material* conditions remained the same with respect to
Soviet power, the decision-making elites in other states perceived the
Soviet Union to be fundamentally different. And thus, they perceived
the entire structure of power relations to be fundamentally different.

In short, "the structure" was what these decision-making elites believed
it to be. Moreover, this belief was reflected not merely in verbal claims
by the rest of the world; the actions of statespersons—changes
in military preparedness and targeting policies, altering of defense
bureaucracies, and so on—demonstrated that this belief was validated
by behavior.

While it is true that different states may perceive structure differently, I believe that there can be intersubjective meaning. Despite arguments by Professor Bozeman and others, I would assert that shared
understandings do, in fact, develop. This is not to say that there is one,
universal philosophical framework; nor is it necessarily to claim that
there are things that all individuals can know through reason. Rather,
as human beings interact with one another, things can take on common meanings. It is in the process of communicating and behaving
that "structure" or "conditions" begin to mean similar things to individual decision makers. A fork, for example, takes on the meaning of
an eating utensil as people use it as such and others see it being used as
such. This same common meaning can obtain at the level of international politics. The cold war existed because decision-making elites in
states throughout the world responded in a more or less similar way
to material conditions in the system. The cold war ended as these individuals nearly uniformly changed their response. There was, I believe, a shared understanding of the power structure.

In support of this notion of shared meaning, I believe that international legal rules provide clear examples. While there may, at present,
be disagreement about the meaning of "human rights" or "aggression"
or "the common heritage of humankind," many international legal
concepts have acquired shared meaning through state interactions over
the centuries. A few examples can illustrate. First, and at the most basic
level, there seems to be general agreement about what the word "state"
as a juridical concept means. Scholars and practitioners may differ about
whether a particular entity is a state, but they would almost universally acknowledge that there is such a thing as a state. Moreover, they
would recognize that states are the building blocks of the international
system—the primary actors. Second, there seems to be little controversy over what "jurisdiction" as a legal concept means. It is the right
of a state to assert its authority over an individual, other legal person,

or in connection with a thing or event.[144] While different states may have conflicting views over when a particular state has jurisdiction, the *concept* of jurisdiction itself is shared. No spokesperson for a state would doubt the existence of the notion of "jurisdiction." Third, I would submit—and indeed have already indicated—that there is universal agreement on the concept of "international law" itself. In other words, the decision-making elites throughout the world recognize that there is such a thing as international law. They believe that there are distinctively "legal rules" that are binding on international actors. Once again, there may be disagreement about the content of particular legal rules, but there would not be disagreement with the notion that there is something called "international law" or "international legal rules."[145] Nor, I would argue, is there disagreement that international law at present is created primarily by states.

My second argument for constructivism is that I believe the identities and interests of states can undergo change through the process of interaction. Certainly, the decision-making elites of states generally engage in rational calculations to realize the basic goals of their state. But how a state defines its goals depends upon how the state understands its identity. And identity is shaped by interaction with other states.

In support of this proposition, it seems clear that participation in *legal* regimes has, in fact, altered the identities of states over the years. One example may be the nuclear non-proliferation regime. Following the advent of the nuclear age, possession of a nuclear weapon became a membership card to an elite club. States would clearly gain status— and thus a particular identity—in the international system by joining this club. As efforts were made to limit the proliferation of nuclear weapons,[146] many states began to see the advantages of adhering to the non-proliferation regime.[147] Over time, as states continued to participate in this regime, it seems reasonable to assert that they began to see themselves as "nonnuclear" states. Sweden, for example, began efforts in 1945 to establish a nuclear weapons program.[148] After much debate, it decided that such a program would not be in its interest[149] and then went on to sign the NPT.[150] By now, it is more than likely that Sweden sees itself as a "nonnuclear" state. Under this logic, it would not go nuclear, even though it possesses the capability,[151] because this would be contrary to its identity. The legal regime, it would seem, played a critical role in forging this change of identity.[152]

In sum, constructivism does seem to provide the most useful framework for understanding the dynamics of international relations. While both structural realism and rationalist institutionalism have certain explanatory power, constructivism seems to give both scholars and practitioners a more accurate description of the international system. Constructivism recognizes that the international system is socially constructed. And it acknowledges the role that structure plays in altering the identity of the actors.

LEGAL RULES AND INTERNATIONAL POLITICS

Given these advantages to a constructivist understanding of international relations, what conclusions can be offered about the relationship of international legal rules to international politics? Here I would like to set out several points about the role of international legal rules in the international system. In some respects, this section will summarize some of the points that were made above; in other respects it will elaborate upon the previous discussion. In elaborating upon these conclusions, I wish to note that these points are by no means the definitive conclusions about legal rules and international politics. As research continues in this area, these conclusions, I hope, will be enlarged and expanded.

[handwritten margin note: disclaimer]

1. International Legal Rules Are Socially Constructed

The first conclusion is that international legal rules are socially constructed. Indeed, as Professor Robert Beck has noted,[153] international legal rules are perhaps one of the best examples of something that is socially constructed. As noted throughout this book, legal rules are created by authoritative state practice. They are not "things" that exist "out there." A putative rule is law if states believe that rule to be authoritative and the rule has control. This is merely another way of saying that legal rules are socially constructed. The rules take on their

[handwritten margin note: Constructed by authoritative state practice]

significance as legal rules as states come to believe them to be law and act according to that belief. A legal rule prohibiting slave trade is created when states come to recognize that prohibition to have a legal character and refuse to engage in slave trade.

2. International Legal Rules
Have Intersubjective Meaning

A second conclusion about international legal rules is that they have shared meaning. Again, as Professor Beck has pointed out,[154] for the concept of authority, or, to use the traditional term, *opinio juris*, to be significant, there must be intersubjective meaning. There can be no legal rule without shared expectations of authority. Indeed, I would assert that the very existence of legal rules proves that there can be intersubjective meaning. As noted above, this conclusion does not mean that every conceivable putative legal rule reflects this shared meaning. I do not believe, for example, that there is shared meaning on the exact contours of the concept of "aggression."[155] But I do believe that there are shared understandings about most of the vast corpus of international legal rules.

3. International Legal Rules Constitute the
Structure of the International System

A third conclusion is that international legal rules do, in part, constitute the structure of the international system. In an earlier section, "Constructivism and International Legal Rules," I explored how Professor Stephen Kocs advances this argument and the specific ways in which he believes international law constitutes the structure of the system. Drawing upon Kocs and others and some of my earlier discussion, I would like to present several propositions about how I believe international legal rules constitute the structure of the system.

First, international law enshrines the doctrine of sovereignty. The concept of sovereignty—the notion that states are independent, that they can be bound by no higher law without their consent, that they are juridically equal—is one of the fundamental assumptions underlying international relations. While I agree with the standard caveats about the notion of sovereignty—it may not be absolute, it may undergo change, it can be distinguished from empirical autonomy,[156]—the concept forms a most basic operating principle of international affairs. It is ingrained in the minds of all international actors and can be considered one of the primary building blocks of the modern international system.

Second, and inextricably related to the first point, international law establishes the criteria for membership in the international system. It determines when a particular international actor will enjoy certain rights and duties at the global level. International law, for example, establishes the criteria for statehood. It determines when an entity can be regarded as a state. In so doing, international law confers legitimacy on states. International legal rules also determine when nonstate actors will be endowed with rights and duties. It determines, for example, when an international organization can enter into international agreements and when the decision of such an organization can be binding on members.

Third, international law provides rules that determine when other legal rules will be binding.[157] In other words, international law contains "general principles about the nature of international law." These constitute the international system because they serve as the bases of the entire legal system. As noted in chapter 2, principles such as the notion that legal rules are created through state consent, that agreements are to be carried out (*pacta sunt servanda*), and so on are the fundamental assumptions upon which the contemporary system of international law is based. Without shared acceptance of these principles, there would be no international legal system as we know it.

Fourth, international law provides a language for diplomacy. As Nigel Purvis, commenting on the New Stream of international legal scholarship, observes, "on the most basic level, sovereigns seem to take for granted the propriety of engaging in international legal discourse (instead of some other type of discourse) when they seek to resolve international issues."[158] When international actors speak, they use the idiom of international law. Decision-making elites in states assert their positions in terms of legal rights. They make *legal* claims. When, for instance, a state decides to use armed force, it will invariably present its claim in terms of international law. It is rare indeed for a state to justify its actions based solely on political, practical, or even moral factors.[159] Some reference to legal principles is made in virtually every case. When the United States invaded Grenada in 1983,[160] or Argentina seized the Falkland Islands (Islas Malvinas) in 1982,[161] or Iraq moved into Kuwait in 1990,[162] these states justified their actions in legal terms.

Likewise, if a state is critical of the behavior of another state, it will frequently castigate that state for failure to abide by its *legal* obligations. Many states criticized the system of apartheid in South Africa as a violation of international human rights law; the United States accused the Soviet Union of violating the Anti-Ballistic Missile Treaty—a legally binding international agreement—by establishing a Phased-Array Radar at Krasnoyarsk.

Fifth, international law gives normative value to actions and claims made by international actors. As Friedrich Kratochwil notes, the international legal order "specifies the steps necessary to insure the validity of their official acts and assigns weight and priority to different claims."[163] In other words, when states or other international actors contemplate a particular action, legal rules provide guidance about what procedure to follow in order for the act to be perceived to be legitimate. During the Gulf War, for example, international law provided a procedure that the United States and its allies could use to ensure that the action against Iraq would receive the maximum degree of legitimacy. By using the process set forth in Chapter VII of the United Nations Charter, the United States did as much as possible to avoid the charge of unilateralism. In addition, once a state or other international actor has acted, international legal rules make certain normative judgments about the legitimacy of the action. Thus, when Iran denied immunity of diplomats from the United States, the act was perceived to be legally "wrong." Similarly, when the United Nations sent peacekeeping troops into Cambodia to supervise a transition to power, other international actors believed that action to be legally "right."

4. The Effect of Legal Rules on the Identity and Interests of States Is Susceptible to Empirical Testing

As noted earlier, one of the criticisms that can be raised against constructivism relates to the mutually constitutive relationship between agent and structure. If each is constantly affecting the other, how can one determine "which is doing what to which" at any point in time? While this problem does not completely disappear with legal rules, I believe that it becomes less troublesome. Legal rules are identifiable parts of the structure of the international system, unlike, perhaps, other types of rules or norms. This is true for several reasons. First, as noted earlier, the decision-making elites in all states—and indeed in almost all other nonstate actors—acknowledge the existence of something called "international law." Second, as discussed in chapter 2, there is nearly universal acceptance of the process by which a putative rule becomes international law. Third, and as a consequence of this second point, it is much easier to determine when a legal rule has come into being than it is to determine when some other type of rule or element of the structure has come into existence. This is especially true for rules established by convention. Scholars do not, for example, disagree about when the 1972 Anti-Ballistic Missile Treaty entered into force. With rules of customary international law, it may be more difficult to pinpoint the precise beginning of the legal rule. Nonetheless, because there is a great deal of agreement about the criteria required for a rule of customary international law, scholars can probably still be more accurate than with other types of rules. Even though not all scholars would agree on the exact date of the emergence of a rule of customary international law providing for innocent passage through territorial sea, there would be broad agreement that after a certain general time period such a rule did exist. Fourth, because it is easier to determine the "birthday" of an international legal rule, it is easier to follow changes in the identity and interests of states that result from the rule. Finally, while there continues to be a mutually constitutive relationship between states and international legal rules—the identity of states can be changed by the rule *and* the rule can change through state practice—there are clear criteria to determine when the rule itself has changed. As a consequence, legal rules provide an excellent yardstick for examining the effect of an important element of the social structure of the international system on the identities and interests of states. In the environmental field, for example, a scholar could observe the creation of legal rules prohibiting the production of certain greenhouse gases. One could determine at what point these rules became authoritative and controlling. From that point, the scholar could then examine the behavior of states—public statements, domestic laws, enforcement of laws—to explore changes that might be taking place in the identities of states.

5. International Legal Rules Change the Identity and Interests of States

A final conclusion about the role international legal rules play in international politics is that legal rules *can* change the identity of states, and, accordingly, change the interests of states. Earlier the example of the nuclear non-proliferation regime was given. Two examples will be explored here: the 1982 Convention on the Law of the Sea and the European Union. The Law of the Sea process illustrates how a legal regime—even without establishing formal institutions to implement all provisions of the agreement—can affect the identity of actors, whereas the European Union demonstrates how international legal rules do, at times, establish formal international institutions that then affect state identity.

The 1982 Convention on the Law of the Sea

The process surrounding the adoption of the 1982 Law of the Sea Convention[164] is, I believe, a useful example of how a legal regime can alter the identity of states. The effect of this process can be seen at several different levels.

At one level, the Third United Nations Conference on the Law of the Sea (UNCLOS III)[165] and the legal provisions embodied in the Convention may have changed the identity of one of the most powerful negotiating blocs in the Conference: the Group of 77 (G-77).[166] These developing states entered the process with a corporate identity of underdeveloped states that had suffered much at the hands of the Western, developed states. They perceived themselves to have been marginalized, in particular, to have been excluded from the law-creating process. The law that existed at the time the Conference began had been created by Western states to serve the interests of those states.[167] Throughout the Conference, the G-77 states reiterated much of the rhetoric of the so-called New International Economic Order

(NIEO).[168] They wanted, in particular, to establish a procedure for exploiting the resources of the deep seabed that would redress the inequitable distribution that developed during colonialism and give them a real role in the legal regime that was to be established.[169] What the 1982 Convention ultimately did was establish a system of exploiting the seabed that addressed many of the concerns of these under-developed states.[170] Among other things, the Convention provided for significant G-77 participation in the decision-making of the International Seabed Authority[171] and dedicated a share of the proceeds of deep seabed mining to aid development of those states.[172]

This process, it would seem, has begun to significantly alter the identity of these states. During UNCLOS III, these states became empowered. While they did not achieve everything they desired,[173] they accomplished many of their goals, which were ultimately reflected in specific provisions of the Convention. In an interesting way, this positive development has helped change their identity. The states have been enfranchised; they have been given a stake in the legal system for regulating the oceans and their resources. Assuming that the Convention continues to receive ratifications and is put into effect,[174] this new way in which these states perceive themselves will more than likely solidify. Their identity—when compared to 1967 when the whole process began[175]—will have undergone change due to their participation in the law of the sea regime. No longer will these states be able to see themselves as marginalized with respect to the management of ocean resources; they will likely view themselves as enfranchised "players."[176]

At another level, the law of the sea process can be seen as affecting the identity of two very specific groups of states. The first of these consists of archipelagic states.[177] Before UNCLOS III began, the special status of archipelagic states had not been recognized by international law.[178] Nonetheless, these states—like Fiji and Indonesia—believed that they should be given different treatment. As Professor Friedheim explains, "because of the scattering of their populations and territory over numerous islands, they had trouble binding their people together in a cohesive social and political whole, and in enforcing their fishing, sanitary, and fiscal regulations."[179] Moreover, "smuggling was a major problem."[180] These states argued, "that their people were more dependent upon the ocean for their livelihoods than most other states and that, as a consequence, they should be entitled to draw baselines from the outermost points of the outermost islands of their island chains."[181] "Within these baselines," they contended, "all waters would become internal waters, creating an exclusive property right for the archipelago state."[182] Ultimately, the Convention granted these states the right to draw this type of baseline.[183] Within these archipelagic waters, the state would have "sovereignty over the airspace, seabed, and re-sources."[184] While the vessels of other states would enjoy the right to transit archipelagic waters, the archipelagic state would be able to re-strict this transit to certain established "archipelagic sea lanes."[185] The Convention also imposed certain duties and obligations on archipelagic states with respect to states that transit those sea lanes.[186]

How has the legal regime altered the identity of these states? Clearly, the archipelagic nature of a state is an integral part of its identity. To be Fiji, for example, is to be an archipelagic state. While these states had that identity before the legal regime was established, the Conven-tion clarified this identity as a matter of international law. It spelled out exactly what an archipelagic state was. In particular, it established the sovereignty of the archipelagic state over the vast waters between the islands. With the Convention, therefore, the international com-munity recognized a specific legal identity for an archipelagic state. The state was to possess certain concrete legal rights and certain specific obligations.

In the case of archipelagic states, the identity of "archipelagic" existed before the Convention, but, underwent an important alteration. In the case of geographically disadvantaged states, the Conference and thus the Convention may have actually created a new specific identity for states. Geographically disadvantaged states are defined by the Con-vention as coastal states "whose geographical situation makes them dependent upon the exploitation of the living resources of the exclu-sive economic zones of other States in the subregion or region for adequate supplies of fish for nutritional purposes of their populations or parts thereof, and coastal States which can claim no exclusive eco-nomic zones of their own."[187] A geographically disadvantaged state is thus one that does not have the same kinds of benefits from an exclu-sive economic zone that most coastal states do. Either they cannot claim their own economic zone due to the geographic configuration of their coast or they have to rely on the economic zones of other states for access to the resources of this part of the ocean. The Convention goes on to grant specific rights to these disadvantaged states.[188] It is clear that there was no such concept as "geographically disadvantaged states" until efforts began to establish in law a 200-nautical mile exclusive economic zone. As this jurisdictional zone was set up, certain states could then begin to perceive themselves as disadvantaged. The Convention thus established a new identity for certain states. Presumably, as these states continue to interact in the international system, this identity will undergo further change. What it means to be a "geographically disadvantaged state" may mean an additional bundle of rights and obligations.

In all these examples, it would seem that the Law of the Sea Convention has begun the process of identity transformation. Assuming that the legal regimes established in the Convention continue, what it means to be a developing state, an archipelagic state, and a geographical disadvantaged state will have been changed through participation in the legal regime.

The European Union

Another example of the effect of legal rules on the identity of states can be found in the European Union. Unlike the Law of the Sea regime, the European Union is a formal international organization. Thus, it provides an illustration of a case in which international legal rules establish an organization that then, in turn, affects the identity of the member states.

What today is know as the European Union is the result of a long series of international legal agreements that began in the early 1950s. In 1951, the Treaty of Paris established the European Coal and Steel Community, which initially consisted of six states: Belgium, France, the Federal Republic of Germany, Italy, Luxembourg, and the Netherlands.[189] A few years later, in 1957, two Treaties of Rome established the European Economic Community and the European Atomic Energy Community.[190] In 1965, the so-called Merger Treaty was adopted—the Treaty Establishing a Single Council and a Single Commission of the European Communities.[191] "By 1986," as John

McCormick reports, "EEC membership had grown to twelve, and the EEC had become known simply as the European Community (EC)."[192] The following year, the Single European Act entered into force.[193] This act called for the establishment of a "single market" before the end of 1992[194] by removing "most of the remaining physical, fiscal, and technical barriers to the creation of a true common market."[195] Finally, in 1991, the Treaty on European Union was produced at Maastricht and entered into force in 1993.[196] These treaties established the legal framework that undergirds the European Union.

What we have seen over the forty-plus years has been, I would argue, a fundamental shift in the identity of European states. While much of the literature on the European Union has focused on the question of whether the identity of citizens of the respective states has undergone change,[197] there is strong evidence that the identity of the states has undergone change.

When the initial debates over European integration were taking place in the 1950s, Germany and France had particular visions of their national identity.[198] At that time, governmental leaders—Konrad Adenauer and Robert Schuman, in particular—had to work to convince their respective parliaments of the benefits of the European Coal and Steel Community. As Professor Thomas Banchoff reports, "during the early 1950s, opponents of integration underscored its incompatibility with the external dimension of national identity—sovereignty in international affairs."[199] "French opponents of the ECSC," explains Banchoff, "claimed that absolute sovereignty and independence was necessary to prevent a resurgence of aggressive German power, while German opponents warned integration within the ECSC would advance French hegemony."[200] This particular type of opposition, however, was not present during the debates surrounding the ratification of the Maastricht Treaty. As Banchoff explains, "by the 1990s, the experience of four decades of peace in Western Europe had altered received conceptions of national identity."[201] "Even those Gaullists, like [Philippe] Seguin, who opposed any *further* transfers of sovereignty to the EU," continues Banchoff, "did not perceive—or pursue—a Europe of national sovereignties and rivalries akin to that of the interwar period."[202] Seguin "did not advocate the abolition of European institutions already in place."[203] As Banchoff sees it, "for

Maastricht's most influential critic, the reality of the EU constituted a starting point for French policy in Europe."[204]

In short, what has happened to states like France and Germany is what Banchoff calls the "Europeanization of national identity."[205] Over the years since the foundation of formal European institutions, "leading political forces in both Germany and France have increasingly come to view their nations as anchored within European institutions, and to recognize the EU as a legitimate framework for politics."[206] France and Germany are different from what they were in 1950 and, I would argue, the institutions of European integration were crucial in bringing about this change. Thus, legal rules were instrumental in establishing the formal organization that then played a critical role in altering the identity of the states.

In sum, I believe these cases illustrate that legal rules—both those connected with a formal international organization and those not fully connected with such a formal institution—can alter the identity of states. Clearly, much more empirical research needs to take place on these cases and myriad others to explore in greater depth how legal rules can change the identities of states. Such research, I would argue, must necessarily be interdisciplinary in nature—drawing upon the insights of international relations and international law.

CONCLUSION

Given the examination in this chapter of contending international relations theories, I believe that constructivism provides scholars, practitioners, and others with a clearer understanding of the nature of international relations than do other approaches. And with respect to the specific concerns of this book, constuctivism gives us a better explanation of the role legal rules play in international relations. Despite the arguments made by structural realists that international legal rules are epiphenomenal, constructivism demonstrates the significance of international law in the international political arena. Legal rules constitute the structure of the international system. This means that the parameters of the system in which states and other actors find themselves is determined, at least in part, by international law. The playing field, in other words, is defined to a large degree by international legal rules. Moreover, constructivism demonstrates that legal rules can affect the identity of actors in this system. As states develop new rules of international law—either through treaty or custom—their participation in the legal regime may alter their identity. In short, constructivism provides a theoretical foundation for understanding what I believe most legal scholars take for granted about the contribution of legal rules—that international law matters in international politics.

NOTES

1. This is a question that I have been exploring for several years. My first effort came in my chapter in a volume that Robert J. Beck, Robert Vander Lugt, and I edited: Anthony Clark Arend, Toward an Understanding of International Legal Rules, in Robert J. Beck, Anthony Clark Arend & Robert D. Vander Lugt, eds., *International Rules: Approaches from International Law and International Relations* 289–310 (1996). More recently, an earlier draft of this present chapter was revised and published as a law journal article: Anthony Clark Arend, Do Legal Rules Matter? International Law and International Politics, 38 *Va. J. Int'l L.* 107–153. This chapter is an elaboration of these earlier works. It is also interesting to note, that other scholars have been approaching the connection between international relations theory and international law from a similar perspective. While this chapter was being revised, I received Benedict Kingsbury, The Concept of Compliance as a Function of Competing Conceptions of International Law, 19 *Mich. J. Int'l L.* 345–372 (1998). Working independently, we have reached some similar conclusions.

2. I draw from the focus essay Classical Realism, in Robert J. Beck, Anthony Clark Arend & Robert D. Vander Lugt, *International Rules*, at 94.

3. I draw upon Professor Robert J. Lieber's discussion of classical realism. Robert J. Lieber, *No Common Power* 10 (3d ed. 1995).

4. I draw upon the writing of Hans Morgenthau in this brief discussion of classical realism. See Hans J. Morgenthau, *Politics Among Nations: The Struggle for Power and Peace* 3–15 (5th ed., 1978).

5. I will always be indebted to Steven P. Soper for his insights on this issue.

6. See Hans Morgenthau, *Politics Among Nations*.

7. The term "structural realism" is used here to describe a particular school of international relations theory. As Professor Charles L. Glaser notes, "struc-

tural realists are sometimes referred to as neorealists." Charles L. Glaser, Realists as Optimists: Cooperation as Self-Help, 19 *Int'l Security* 50 n. 1 (1994/1995). Moreover, "some authors want to reserve 'neorealism' to refer to the theory as articulated by [Kenneth] Waltz, while using structural realism to refer to a broader family of systemic theories." Id.

8. Of course, two primary structural realist assumptions are not mentioned by Mearsheimer, but clearly underlie his analysis. These are the following. First, states are the primary actors in the international system. Second, states behave as unitary actors. See, Charles L. Glaser, Realists as Optimists, at 54–55.

9. John J. Mearsheimer, The False Promise of International Institutions, 19 *Int'l Security* 5, 10 (1994/1995).

10. Id.

11. Id.

12. Robert J. Lieber, *No Common Power*, at 5.

13. This is the title of Professor Lieber's book.

14. John J. Mearsheimer, The False Promise, at 10.

15. Id.

16. Id.

17. Id.

18. Id.

19. Id.

20. Hans J. Morgenthau, *Politics Among Nations*, at 10.

21. John J. Mearsheimer, The False Promise, at 10.

22. Id.

23. Id. at 11.

24. Id.

25. Id.

26. Id.

27. Id.

28. Id.

29. Id. at 11–12.

30. See Joseph M. Grieco, Anarchy and the Limits of Cooperation: A Realist Critique of the Newest Liberal Institutionalism, 42 *Int'l Organization* 498–500 (1988).

31. Kenneth Waltz, *Theory of International Politics* 126 (1979).

32. Hans Morgenthau, *Politics Among Nations*, at 279.

33. George F. Kennan, *American Diplomacy* 95 (Expanded ed., 1984).

34. A notable exception is Robert J. Lieber. He devotes several sections of his book, *No Common Power*, to an examination of international law. He concludes that "the actual practices of states, far more than codified treaties and

agreements, thus do constitute a rudimentary but nonetheless real body of international law." Robert J. Lieber, *No Common Power*, at 292.

35. Susan Strange, *Cave! hic dragones:* A Critique of Regime Analysis, in 36 *Int'l Organization* 337, 345 (1982).

36. Stephen D. Krasner, Structural Causes and Regime Consequences: Regimes as Intervening Variables, 36 *Int'l Organization* 1, 6 (1982).

37. Id.

38. Id. at 189.

39. Id.

40. Id.

41. Robert Gilpin, *War and Change in International Politics* 35 (1981). I draw upon Robert J. Beck, International Law and International Relations: The Prospects for Interdisciplinary Collaboration, in Robert J. Beck, Anthony Clark Arend, and Robert D. Vander Lugt, *International Rules*, at 3, 15.

42. In a similar vein, Professor Greico summarized the structural realist position on "institutions," by claiming that "international institutions affect the prospects for cooperation only marginally." Joseph M. Grieco, Anarchy and the Limits of Cooperation, at 488.

43. See, e.g., Robert J. Lieber, *No Common Power*, at 34–88, where he provides a structural realist examination of the cold war.

44. Of the many volumes of literature critical of structural realism, a useful starting place includes the following: David A. Baldwin, ed., *Neorealism and Neoliberalism: The Contemporary Debate* (1993); Robert O. Keohane, ed., *Neorealism and Its Critics* (1985).

45. Alexander Wendt, Constructing International Politics, 20 *Int'l Security* 71, 77–78 (1994/1995).

46. Id. at 78.

47. Id.

48. I am grateful to Professor Joseph Lepgold for helping me phrase this point.

49. As Ronald L. Jepperson argues, "in neorealism states have largely unproblematic—that is, unvarying and contextual—identities and interests." Ronald L. Jepperson, Norms, Identity, and Culture, in Peter J. Katzenstein, ed., *The Culture of National Security: Norms and Identity in World Politics* 33, 43 (1996). Ted Hopf argues that "neorealism assumes that all units in global politics have only one meaningful identity, that of self-interested states." Ted Hopf, The Promise of Constructivism in International Relations Theory, 23 *Int'l Security* 171 (Summer 1998).

50. This is essentially the critique raised by constructivist Alexander Wendt. See Alexander Wendt, Anarchy Is What States Make of It: The Social Con-

struction of Power Politics, in 46 *Int'l Organization* 391 (1992); Alexander Wendt, Constructing International Politics, at 71.

51. Robert O. Keohane, International Institutions: Two Approaches, in 32 *Int'l Studies Quarterly* 379 (1988).

52. Scholars have developed various names to describe approaches in this family. Perhaps the most predominate is "neo-liberal institutionalism." While different scholars would accord different significance to some of these labels, I will choose "rationalist institutionalism" to describe this entire family of approaches that seek to challenge structural realism in a similar way. See Robert J. Beck, Anthony Clark Arend & Robert D. Vander Lugt, Institutionalist Approaches, in *International Rules*, at 165–166. I am indebted to Alexander Wendt for assistance with this terminology.

53. See Robert J. Beck, Anthony Clark Arend, and Robert D. Vander Lugt, eds., *International Rules*, at 165.

54. Robert O. Keohane, International Institutions, at 386.

55. Keohane notes the tendency to think of institutions this way. Robert O. Keohane, International Institutions, at 382–383.

56. Robert O. Keohane, *International Institutions and State Power: Essays in International Relations Theory* 3 (1989).

57. Oran R. Young, *International Cooperation: Building Regimes for Natural Resources and the Environment* 6 (1989).

58. Id. at 5.

59. This discussion draws upon our discussion of the institutionalist approaches in Robert J. Beck, Anthony Clark Arend, and Robert D. Vander Lugt, *International Rules*, at 165. I am particular indebted to Robert Vander Lugt's organization of these concepts.

60. John G. Ruggie, International Response to Technology: Concepts and Trends, 29 *Int'l Organization* 570 (1975).

61. Stephen D. Krasner, Structural Causes and Regime Consequences, at 1, 2.

62. Oran R. Young, *International Cooperation*, at 12.

63. Id. at 12–13.

64. Robert O. Keohane, International Institutions, at 386.

65. Id.

66. For a discussion of the concept of the "shadow of the future," see Robert Axelrod & Robert Keohane, Achieving Cooperation Under Anarchy, in *Neorealism and Neoliberalism*, at 91–94.

67. Robert O. Keohane, International Institutions, at 386.

68. Stephen D. Krasner, Structural Causes and Regime Consequences, at 7–8.

69. Id. at 7.

70. Id. at 8.

71. Id. (footnote omitted).

72. In using the "high politics"–"low politics" distinction, I recognize that these are not absolute categories. Instead, I tend to regard them as poles on a continuum. Some issues—such as nuclear war—are at the high politics end of the spectrum; other issues—such as the exchange of weather information—are at the low politics end. Other issues fall at various points between these two poles. Of course, at different points in time the same issue may be located at different points on the spectrum. Petroleum exportation might be an issue of low politics when oil is in plentiful supply and an issue of high politics when it is scarce. It should also be noted that different states will regard different issues as high or low politics. Water regulation, for example, could be a matter of high politics for an extremely arid state, but a matter of low politics for a tropical state.

73. Ironically, this turn of phrase is borrowed (albeit in a very different context) from the former General Secretary of the Communist Party of the Soviet Union, Yuri Andropov, who once observed: "Any citizen of the Soviet Union whose interests coincide with the interests of society feels the entire scope of our democratic freedoms." *Izvestiia*, June 10, 1975, at 1, quoted in Richard N. Dean, Beyond Helsinki: The Soviet View of Human Rights in International Law, 21 *Va. J. Int'l L.* 55, 63–64 (1980).

74. Robert J. Beck, *The Grenada Invasion: Politics, Law, and Foreign Policy Decisionmaking* 228 n. 9 (1993).

75. Alexander Wendt, Collective Identity Formation and the International State, 88 *American Political Science Review* 384 (1994) See also, Robert Keohane, International Institutions, at 390.

76. As Wendt says more generally, "few [neoliberals] treat state interests as *endogenous* to interaction." Id. "They," he explains, "either bracket the formation of interests, treating them *as if* they were exogenous, or explain interests by reference to domestic politics, on the assumption that they are exogenous, although not necessarily constant." Id. "In both cases," Wendt continues, "the effect on systemic theory is captured by what Jeffrey Legro . . . calls the rationalist 'two-step': first interests are formed outside the interaction context, and then the latter is treated as though it only affected behavior." Id. In short, for the neoliberals "systemic interaction does not transform state interests [or, I would add, state identity]." Id.

77. Robert Keohane, International Institutions, at 389.

78. "Constructivism," it should be noted, is a social theory that has been in existence for some time. Over the past several years, however, the term

has been explicitly applied to international relations. In this work, I will use constructivism to describe that particular approach to international relations. (I am indebted to Professor Wendt for pointing out this distinction to me.)

79. See Alexander Wendt and Raymond Duvall, Institutions and International Order, in Ernst-Otto Czempiel and James N. Rosenau, eds., *Global Changes and Theoretical Challenges* 51–73 (1989) for a discussion of the British approach and its relationship to constructivism.

80. John Gerard Ruggie, *Constructing the World Polity: Essays on International Institutionalism*, 11 (1998).

81. Alexander Wendt, Constructing International Politics, at 71.

82. Id. See also, Alexander Wendt, Collective Identity Formation and the International State, at 384.

83. Id. at 71–72.

84. Ted Hopf, The Promise of Constructivism in International Relations Theory, at 181. What Hopf is essentially asserting here is that critical theory is inevitably postmodern. Constructivism, he seems to claim here, is not postmodern; therefore it cannot be seen to be a variety of critical theory.

85. John Gerard Ruggie, *Constructing the World Polity*, at 35.

86. Id. at 35–36.

87. Id. at 35.

88. Id.

89. Id.

90. In Robert J. Beck, Anthony Clark Arend, & Robert D. Vander Lugt, *International Rules*, at 165–166, I and my colleagues use the term "sociological institutionalism" to describe what amounts to a constructivist approach to international institutions. That term was suggested by Professor Wendt.

91. Alexander Wendt, Constructing International Politics, at 72.

92. Id. at 73.

93. Id.

94. Id.

95. Id.

96. Id. (footnote omitted).

97. Id.

98. Id. at 74.

99. Id.

100. This is reminiscent of the theological discussion of "faith" and "works." An individual can say that he or she believes in God, but if he or she does not live a life consistent with that belief, does that person really believe in God?

101. It should be noted that while some constructivists assume that the structure of the international system exists as an objective reality, they recognize that this structure can only be known in a mediated fashion. As Wendt explains, "all observation is theory-*laden* in the sense that what we see is mediated by our existing theories, and to that extent knowledge is inherently problematic." Id. at 75. "But," he continues, "this does not mean that observation, let alone reality is theory-*determined*." Id. "The world is out there constraining our beliefs," Wendt notes, "and may punish us for incorrect ones." Id.

102. As Professor Ruggie explains:

Constructivists hold the view that the building blocks of international reality are ideational as well as material; that ideational factors have normative as well as instrumental dimensions; that they express not only individual but also collective intentionality; and that the meaning and significance of ideational factors are not independent of time and place.

John Gerard Ruggie, *Constructing the World Polity*, at 33.

103. Alexander Wendt, Anarchy Is What States Make of It, at 46.

104. Id.

105. Id.

106. I am indebted to my colleague Marilyn McMorrow for help in describing this relationship. Another way of thinking about this connection between agent and structure is suggested by my colleague Patricia Wrightson, who calls the relatiohship a dialectic one.

107. Robert Keohane, International Institutions, at 382.

108. Id.

109. Id.

110. See Hedley Bull, *The Anarchical Society* 125–161 (1977).

111. Professor Wendt, for example, mentions international law in several of his articles. See Alexander Wendt, Constructing International Politics, at 76; Alexander Wendt and Raymond Duvall, Institutions and International Order, at 56.

112. Andrew Hurrell, International Society and the Study of Regimes: A Reflective Approach, in Volker Rittberger and Peter Mayer, eds., *Regime Theory and International Relations* 49–72 (1993).

113. Here I am using "institution" in the way in which Keohane uses the term. As noted earlier in the text, he defines institutions as "persistent and connected sets of rules (formal and informal) that prescribe behavior roles, constrain activity, and shape expectations." Robert O. Keohane, *International Institutions and State Power*, at 3. International Law can be thought of as such an

institution. Thus, the institution of International Law is constitutive of the international system.

114. This view has been reflected in the writings of several international relations theorists. One of the most clear articulations of this position has been made by Professor Stephen A. Kocs. See Stephen A. Kocs, Explaining the Strategic Behavior of States: International Law as System Structure, 38 *Int'l Studies Quarterly* 535–556 (1994).

115. Andrew Hurrell, International Society and the Study of Regimes, at 59.

116. Young, for example, uses this analogy. He explains that "it just does not make sense for a chess player to refuse to accept the concept of checkmate, for the speaker of English to assert that it makes no difference whether subjects and predicates agree, or for an actor in the existing international society to disregard the rules regarding the nationality of citizens." Oran R. Young, International Regimes: Toward a New Theory of Institutions, 39 *World Politics*, 104, 120 (1986). Ruggie uses the chess example too. John Gerard Ruggie, *Constructing the Word Polity*, at 22.

117. Friedrich Kratochwil, *Rules, Norms, and Decisions*, 26 (1989).

118. John Rawles, Two Concepts of Rules, 64 *Philosophical Review* 3, 24 (1955).

119. Id.

120. Id.

121. Robert O. Keohane, International Institutions, at 384.

122. Stephen A. Kocs, Explaining the Strategic Behavior of States, at 538.

123. Id.

124. Id. at 539. [Kocs is citing Antonio Cassese, *International Law in a Divided World* 129–157 (1986).]

125. Id.

126. Id.

127. Id.

128. For example, I have argued that the prohibition on the threat or use of force reflected in Article 2(4) of the United Nations Charter is not authoritative and controlling and, therefore, not a principle of contemporary international law. Anthony Clark Arend, International Law and the Recourse to Force: A Shift in Paradigms, 27 *Stan. J. Int'l L.* 1 (1990); Anthony Clark Arend and Robert J. Beck, *International Law and the Use of Force: Beyond the U.N. Charter Paradigm* (1993).

129. Indeed, Kocs himself recognizes that "the precise content of the underlying norms of international law is less important than the fact that such norms exist and that they structure the behavior of states." Stephen Kocs, Explaining the Strategic Behavior of States, at 539.

130. Ruggie discusses regulatory rules in a domestic setting, using the example of traffic law. He explains that "specifying which side of the road to drive on is an example of a regulative rule; as the term implies, it regulates an antecedently existing activity." John Gerard Ruggie, *Constructing the World Polity*, at 22.

131. I draw upon some of Kocs's discussion of international law and state interests.

132. As noted above, this is the thesis of Anthony Clark Arend & Robert J. Beck, *International Law and the Use of Force*, and Anthony Clark Arend, International Law and the Recourse to Force, at 45–47. This is obviously a controversial conclusion. My purpose here is not to reopen this debate, but rather to use claims about the status of Article 2(4) as an example to illustrate the effect that a legal rule could have on the identity of actors.

133. This is a common criticism. See John J. Mearsheimer, A Realist Reply, 20 *Int'l Security* 82, 92 (1995), where Mearsheimer replies to Wendt's critique of Mearsheimer's earlier article.

134. Martha Finnemore, International Organizations as Teachers of Norms: the United Nations Education, Scientific, and Cultural Organization and Science Policy, 47 *Int'l Organization* 565 (1993). Finnemore explains that her "findings . . . lend support to constructivist or reflective theoretical approaches that treat states as social entities, shaped in part by international social action." Id. at 566. "State policies and structures in this case," she explains, "are influenced by changing intersubjective understandings about the appropriate role of the modern state." Id. Her argument about UNESCO is also made in Martha Finnemore, *National Interests in International Society* 34–68 (1996).

135. Martha Finnemore, Constructing Norms of Humanitarian Intervention, in Peter J. Katzenstein, ed., *The Culture of National Security: Norms and Identity in World Politics* 153 (1996).

136. In response to Mearsheimer, Wendt argues that "there is now a substantial body of constructivist empirical work that embodies a wholly conventional epistemology." Alexander Wendt, Constructing International Politics, at 73. Some of the work to which Wendt points include Michael Barnett, Institutions, Roles, and Disorder, 37 *Int'l Studies Quarterly* 271 (1993); David Lumsdaine, *Moral Vision in International Politics* (1993). Professor Ruggie has also pointed to further empirical constructivist works:

> Constructivist empirical studies documenting the impact of principled beliefs on patterns of international outcomes include, among other subjects, the evolution of the human rights regime (Forsythe 1991 [David Forsythe, *The Internationalization of Human Rights*]; Sikkink 1993 [Kathryn

Sikkink, Human Rights, Principled Issue-Networks, and Sovereignty in Latin America, 47 *Int'l Organization* 411–441]), . . . decolonization (Jackson 1993 [Robert Jackson, The Weight of Ideas in Decolonization: Normative Change in International Relations, in J. Goldstein & R.O. Keohane, eds., *Ideas and Foreign Policy*]), and international support for the termination of apartheid (Klotz 1995 [Audie Klotz, *Norms in International Relations: the Struggle Against Apartheid*]); as well as the already mentioned studies on increasingly nondiscriminatory humanitarian interventions (Finnemore 1996c [Martha Finnemore, Constructing Norms of Humanitarian Intervention, in Peter J. Katzenstein, ed., *The Culture of National Security*], the emergence of weapons taboos (Price 1995 [R. Price, A Genealogy of the Chemical Weapons Taboo, 49 *Int'l Organization* 73–103]; Price and Tannenwald 1996 [R. Price & N. Tannenwald, Norms and Deterrence: The Nuclear and Chemical Weapons Taboo, in *The Culture of National Security*]), and the role of multilateral norms in stabilizing the consequences of rapid international change (Chapter 4 [of Ruggie's *Constructing the World Polity*]).

John Gerard Ruggie, *Constructing the World Polity*, at 19. My textual discussion reflects Ruggie's mention of these works.

137. Audie Klotz, *Norms in International Relations: The Struggle Against Apartheid* (1995).

138. I am indebted to my colleague Robert J. Beck for pointing to this concern.

139. Adda Bozeman, *The Future of Law in a Multicultured World* 35–36, 162–178 (1971).

140. To this point, I should add another important caveat. A radical constructivist might be inclined to say that *all things* are socially constructed—things like good and evil, and human nature itself. This is reminiscent of Hamlet's exchange with Rosencrantz and Guildenstern:

Hamlet:	Denmark's a prison.
Rosencrantz:	Then is the world one.
Hamlet:	A goodly one: in which there are many confines, wards and dungeons, Denmark being one of the worst.
Rosencrantz:	We think not so, my lord.
Hamlet:	Why, then, 'tis none to you; *for there is nothing either good or bad, but thinking makes it so*: to me it is a prison.

William Shakespeare, *Hamlet*, Act II, Sc. ii, reprinted in Hardin Craig, *Shakespeare* 735, 754 (1931) (emphasis added). While I believe that the structure of the international system takes on meaning largely as actors interact with one another, I do believe that "good" and "bad" and human nature are not absolute social constructs. Just as one cannot pretend that oceans are not oceans, certain fundamentals of reality cannot be constructed away.

141. Alexander Wendt, Constructing International Politics, at 78.

142. Id.

143. Professor Wendt explains that

the Cold War was a social structure in virtue of which the United States and the USSR had certain identities. These were embodied in "national security worldviews" (in terms of which each defined self and other) and in role positions in a social structure. . . . The content of national interests was in part a function of these structurally constituted identities (as well as of domestic ones).

Alexander Wendt, Collective Identity Formation and the International State, at 386. See also, Rey Koslowski & Friedrich V. Kratochwil, Understanding Change in International Politics: The Soviet Empire's Demise and the International System, 48 *Int'l Organization* 215–247 (1994).

144. See *Restatement of Foreign Relations Law of the United States* (Third), secs. 402, 421, & 431.

145. I would argue that these shared meanings are also influenced by the "epistemic community" of international lawyers. As Professor Peter Haas explains, the term epistemic community "has been used in the literature on sociology of knowledge and has been adapted for use in international relations to refer to a specific community of experts sharing a belief in a common set of cause-and-effect relationships as well as common values to which policies governing these relationships will be applied." Peter Haas, Do Regimes Matter? Epistemic Communities and Mediterranean Pollution Control, reprinted in Friedrich Kratochwil and Edward Mansfield, *International Organization: A Reader* 128, 138 n. 13. Throughout the world, individuals trained in international law occupy important positions in foreign ministries, defense ministries, and in other executive positions. These individuals share an understanding of the nature of international law and, I believe, value the importance of international law as an instrument for the promotion of international order. See Hedley Bull, *The Anarchical Society*, at 136.

146. The most important of these efforts was the conclusion of the Nuclear Non-Proliferation Treaty [NPT]. Treaty on the Non-Proliferation of Nuclear Weapons, opened for signature July 1, 1968, 21 U.S.T. 483, 729 U.N.T.S. 161. For general works on the NPT and the non-proliferation issue, see Lloyd Jensen, *Return from the Nuclear Brink: National Interest and the Nuclear Nonproliferation*

Treaty (1974); Mohamed I. Shaker, *The Nuclear Non-Proliferation Treaty: Origins and Implementation 1959–1979* (1980).

147. In a 1985 publication of the Committee on International Security and Arms Control, it was stated:

> The adherence of more than 120 states to treaties designed to support non-proliferation and the willingness of these states to pay the price of forswearing the future option of acquiring nuclear explosives demonstrates the widespread recognition of the international security advantages of a non-proliferation regime. Significantly, these states include most of the non-nuclear weapons states that could easily develop nuclear weapons. In each case, the states independently concluded that it would be against its overall security interests to undertake such a program or even maintain an option to do so.

Committee on International Security and Arms Control, *Nuclear Arms Control: Background and Issues* 227 (1985).

148. For a discussion of Sweden's program, see Kathleen C. Bailey, *Doomsday Weapons in the Hands of Many: The Arms Control Challenge of the '90s* 30–33 (1991).

149. As the Committee on International Security and Arms Control explain: "Sweden built up such capabilities and seriously debated initiating a weapons program in the 1960s, but finally decided that this would be counter to its security interests." Committee on International Security and Arms Control, *Nuclear Arms Control*, at 233. Kathleen C. Bailey, *Doomsday Weapons in the Hands of Many*, at 30–33.

150. As Dr. Bailey explains: "After Sweden signed the NPT, it abandoned nuclear weapons research except for a limited program of 'protection research.'" Bailey, Doomsday Weapons in the Hands of Many, at 33.

151. Bailey argues that "there is little doubt that Sweden has the technical infrastructure and capability to produce a nuclear explosive if it chooses to do so." Id.

152. I am grateful to Ambassador Thomas Graham for suggesting the role of the NPT in restraining the behavior of states. Mr. Graham has served as the General Counsel and Acting Director for the Arms Control and Disarmament Agency. He was the American representative to the 1995 NPT Extension Conference.

153. Remarks of Robert J. Beck, University of Virginia, November 27, 1994.

154. Id.

155. I would assert that there is a core understanding of what aggression is—an overt attack whose purpose is pure territorial aggrandizement. But beyond that, I believe there are multiple understandings of the concept of

aggression. See Anthony Clark Arend and Robert J. Beck, *International Law and the Use of Force*, at 178–188.

156. As Keohane explains: "As a legal concept, the principle of sovereignty should not be confused with the empirical claim that a given state in fact makes its decisions autonomously." Robert O. Keohane, International Institutions, at 385.

157. Or as Professor Kocs notes in a passage cited earlier in the text, there are legal rules that "exist . . . as a set of underlying, implicit rules which create a framework that allows formal agreements between states to be meaningful and binding." Stephen A. Kocs, Explaining the Strategic Behavior of States, at 538.

158. Nigel Purvis, Critical Legal Studies in Public International Law, 32 *Harv. J. Int'l L.* 110 (1991).

159. An excellent study of such use of international law to justify a particular foreign policy action is Robert J. Beck, *The Grenada Invasion*.

160. See Robert J. Beck, *The Grenada Invasion*.

161. See Alberto R. Coll, Philosophical and Legal Dimensions of the Use of Force in the Falklands War, in Alberto R. Coll & Anthony C. Arend, eds., *The Falklands War: Lessons for Strategy, Law and Diplomacy* 39 (1985).

162. See excerpts from Iraq's Statement on Kuwait, *Washington Post*, Aug. 9, 1990, A18, col. 1.

163. Friedrich V. Kratochwil, *Rules, Norms, and Decisions*, at 251.

164. These concrete examples were suggested by my colleague Professor Charles E. Pirtle, who is an expert on the law of the sea.

165. Much has been written about UNCLOS III. See, e.g., Robert L. Friedheim, *Negotiating the New Ocean Regime* (1993); C. Sanger, *Ordering the Oceans: The Making of the Law of the Sea* (1987); Kenneth R. Simmonds, ed., *The UN Convention on the Law of the Sea* (1983); Philip Allott, Power Sharing in the Law of the Sea 77 *Am. J. Int'l L.* 1 (1983).

166. The Group of 77 was first established at the 1964 United Nations Conference on Trade and Development (UNCTAD) as a "caucusing group" for developing states. Thomas G. Weiss, David P. Forsythe & Roger A. Coate, *The United Nations and Changing World Politics* 183 (1994). At the time of the Conference, there were 77 states that participated. Even though the number of the states belonging to the group increased, the name stayed the same.

167. As Bernard Oxman has explained:

Newly independent countries did not feel any particular commitment to efforts to articulate customary or conventional international law undertaken without their participation. Many associated existing rules of international law, particularly freedom of the seas, with colonial expansionism.

Bernard H. Oxman, Law of the Sea, in Christopher C. Joyner, ed., *The United Nations and International Law*, 319 (1997).

168. See Declaration on the Establishment of a New International Economic Order, G.A. Res. 3201, 6th Spec. Sess. U.N. GAOR Supp. (No. 1), U.N. Doc. A/9559 (1974)(setting forth some of the basic premises of the New International Economic Order). See also, Gillian White, A New International Economic Order? 16 *Va. J. Int'l L.* 323 (1976). I also appreciate the insight of Professor Ibrahim J. Wani on this point.

169. As one commentator observed in 1984:

The movement to create the NIEO is part of the "great debate" between the LDC's [Less Developed Countries] and the developed industrialized nations. Instead of simply trying to prevent renewed colonialism and exploitation of the Third World, the LDC's (represented by the group of 77) are aiming at a major reorganization and redistribution of global wealth. The best vehicles to implement these policies have been in areas of relatively unsettled international law—the oceans and outerspace.

Robert L. Brooke, The Current Legal Status of Deep Seabed Mining, 24 *Va. J. Int'l L.* 379 n. 87 (1984).

170. Part XI of the Convention deals with exploitation of the deep seabed. See 1982 Convention on the Law of the Sea, arts. 133–191.

171. The Convention itself provided for a Council to serve as "the Executive organ of the Authority." Id. art. 162, para. 1. The Council was to consist of 36 members, at least 8 of which were less developed states. Id., art. 161. Before the Convention entered into force, however, a special implementation agreement was concluded. Agreement Relating to the Implementation of Part XI of the United Nations Convention on the Law of the Sea of 10 December 1982, U.N. GAOR, 48th Sess., 101st plen. mtg., Annex, U.N. Doc. A/RES/ 48/263/Annex (1994), reprinted in 33 I.L.M. 1309, Annex at 1313 (1994). This Agreement effectively amends the Convention. See Jonathan I. Charney, Entry Into Force of the 1982 Convention on the Law of the Sea, 35 *Va. J. Int'l L.* 381 (1995). The Agreement also guarantees 8 developing states, although it is likely that there will be more such states. Agreement, sec. 15.

172. Law of the Sea Convention, art. 140.

173. Professor Friedheim attempts to evaluate how well the various negotiating positions fared at the Conference and in the Convention itself. Robert L. Friedheim, *Negotiating the New Ocean Regime*, at 220–263, 289–359.

174. The Convention entered into force on November 16, 1994. The United States and a number of other developed states have yet to ratify the Conven-

tion. Status of the United Nations Convention on the Law of the Sea of 10 December 1982, http://www.un.org/Depts/los/los94st.htm As of January 5, 1999, there were 130 parties to the Convention.

175. For an overview of the beginning of the process, *see* Robert L. Friedheim, *Negotiating the New Ocean Regime*, at 27–31. I am using 1967—the date the United Nations General Assembly created the Ad Hoc Committee on the Peaceful Use of the Seabed and the Ocean Floor Beyond the Limits of National Jurisdiction—as the beginning of the Law of the Sea process. Id. at 30.

176. It could be argued that in light of the 1994 Agreement, the developing states lost many of the rights they had gained in the Convention itself. While it is true that the Agreement accommodated many of the concerns about the Convention that had been raised by the United States and other developed states, the developing states are still strongly behind the Agreement. Jonathan I. Charney, Entry Into Force of the 1982 Convention on the Law of the Sea, at 440 ("One would expect that the major sources of objections [to the Agreement] might come from the developing states, but the Group of 77 supports the Agreement.") (footnote omitted).

177. Under the Convention an "archipelagic state" is "a State constituted wholly by one or more archipelagos and may include other islands." Law of the Sea Convention, art. 46. An "archipelago" is "a group of islands, including parts of islands, interconnecting waters and other natural features which are so closely interrelated that such islands, waters and other natural features form an intrinsic geographical, economic and political entity, or which historically have been regarded as such." Id.

178. Friedheim explains that "until UNCLOS III, archipelago states had claimed, in vain, a need for a special legal status for the waters between their islands." Robert L. Friedheim, *Negotiating the New Ocean Regime*, at 278. For an excellent discussion of some of the problems of archipelagic states and the issue of archipelagic sea-lanes, see J. Peter A. Bernhardt, The Right of Archipelagic Sea Lanes Passage: A Primer, 35 *Va. J. Int'l L.* 719 (1995).

179. Robert L. Friedheim, *Negotiating the New Ocean Regime*, at 278.

180. Id.

181. Id.

182. Id.

183. Law of the Sea Convention, art 47.

184. Robert L. Friedheim, *Negotiating the New Ocean Regime*, at 278. Law of the Sea Convention, art. 49.

185. Law of the Sea Convention, art 53. As Friedheim explains:

But the principal use right of concern to nonarchipelagic states was the right to transit through the waters between some of the major islands of archipelagos. While transitors did not retain the right to roam wherever they pleased, archipelagic states were required to create sea-lanes so that major shipping routes would not be impaired (Article 53). Within archipelagic sea-lanes, transitors would enjoy all the rights of transit passage—and all of its obligations (Article 54).

Robert L. Friedheim, *Negotiating the New Ocean Regime*, at 278.

186. Law of the Sea Convention, art. 53.

187. Id., art. 70, para. 2.

188. Id., art. 70.

189. John McCormick, *The European Union: Politics and Policies* 49–50 (1996).

190. Id. at 52.

191. Id. at 54.

192. Id. at 64.

193. Id. at 69.

194. Id.

195. Id. at 70.

196. Id. at 74–76.

197. See, for example, Paul Taylor, *The European Union in the 1990s* 140–177 (1996). Taylor reviews numerous polls about individuals' attitudes about the European Union.

198. For this discussion, I draw upon Thomas Banchoff, National Identity and EU Legitimacy in France and Germany, in Thomas Banchoff & Michael P. Smith, eds., *Legitimacy and the European Union: The Contested Polity* (forthcoming, 1999) (manuscript version).

199. Id. at 21.

200. Id.

201. Id.

202. Id. (emphasis added).

203. Id. at 18.

204. Id. (reference omitted).

205. Id. at 22.

206. Id. Banchoff begins this sentence: "With the exception of extremist parties on the right and the left." Id.

FIVE

THE FUTURE OF
THE INTERNATIONAL
LEGAL SYSTEM

The preceding chapters of this book have attempted to present several basic propositions about international legal rules in the contemporary international system. First, I have contended that international legal rules are distinctive; they are perceived by the decision-making elites in states to be qualitatively different from other types of rules. Second, I have argued that these legal rules are created by states through their consent. As a consequence, I have developed a methodology for determining when that consent has been given. Third, I have sought to demonstrate that legal rules matter—that they play a critical role in international politics. All these propositions are based on the assumption that the international system remains essentially as it has been for the past several hundred years—an anarchic system in which states are the primary actors. But, as noted in the introduction to this book, the international system has been subjected to unprecedented developments since the end of the cold war. I believe that the *fundamental* nature of this system has not yet changed. It is still a system of sovereign states. Nonetheless, the trajectory of some of these recent developments could indeed indicate that the future—indeed perhaps the very near future—may hold such fundamental systemic changes.

The purpose of this chapter is to explore alternative scenarios for the future of the international system and the implications that these alternatives could have on legal rules. While there are undoubtedly an infinite variety of ways in which the international system could move over the next half century or so, I will limit the discussion here to two plausible scenarios.[1] First, it is conceivable that as time passes there may be a greater centralization of the system. Global multilateral organizations—the United Nations in particular—may come to play a much greater role in international politics and the creation of legal rules. Second, with the rise of a variety of nonstate actors, the international system could become what Hedley Bull has called a "neomedieval" system, where states are but one actor alongside several others and there is "overlapping authority and multiple loyalty."[2] Sections one and two of this chapter will explore these two scenarios and examine their implications for the development of international legal rules. Each section will conclude with an assessment of the likelihood that this scenario will happen. Section three will serve as a conclusion to the chapter.

SCENARIO ONE:
INCREASED CENTRALIZATION

With the demise of the cold war and the successful United Nations efforts against Iraq during the Gulf War, cries went up from many sectors of the globe that we were witnessing the emergence of a "New World Order." Even American President George Bush employed this term to describe what he believed to be the emerging international system. While this phrase itself has been used in a variety of ways, one element that seems to have figured prominently in the "New World Order" literature is the notion of an enhanced role for multilateral organizations.[3] Somehow in this New World Order, unilateral behavior would begin to take a backseat to collective action. In particular, many commentators began to assert that the United Nations Security Council—the body formally charged by its members with the management of international peace and security—would be able to assume a role resembling that provided for in the United Nations Charter. With the end of the deadlock produced by the East-West conflict, the veto no longer seemed to be the obstacle that it had been during the cold war. Indeed, observers could point to the remarkable agreement of the Soviet Union and acquiescence of China that allowed the Security Council to adopt an unprecedented series of resolutions authorizing collective action against Iraq as a harbinger for the future.[4] Even in the conflicts in Cambodia, Somalia, and the Balkans, a surprising degree of cooperation was reflected in the actions of the Security Council. As time passed, however, these hopes seemed to be unfounded. The seeming inability of the United Nations to resolve the conflicts in the Balkans and elsewhere began to give rise to criticism of the world organization. To some, the organization was returning to politics as usual. The apparent successes of the organization were aberrations. There would be no New World Order with the United Nations at the forefront. The system would remain anarchic and decentralized in the extreme.

And yet despite these and other recent criticisms of the United Nations, it remains the case that the organization is playing an unprecedented role in international politics. It is engaged as a major actor in international politics. As of November 1998, the United Nations was sponsoring 16 peace operations throughout the world, involving more than 14,000 troops, observers, and other personnel.[5] Moreover, not only is the United Nations playing an unprecedented role in the management of international conflict, it and other related organizations are also becoming increasingly active in addressing problems of the global commons—the environment, the law of the sea, and other resource issues. If this behavior continues and strengthens, international organizations could have a profound effect on the nature of the international system, which, in turn, would fundamentally affect how international law is created. How could this future play itself out?

In the foreseeable future, two major developments are plausible. First, the centralization trend, if it continues, could lead to the development of a global organization that actually is responsible for the managing of international conflict. The United Nations, through the organ of the Security Council, could truly assume primary responsibility for the maintenance of international peace and security. This would be a far, far cry from the vision of World Federalists or Confederalists. There would be no world legislature or executive body in the domestic sense. States would remain the primary actors in the international system, but would act cooperatively through the United Nations. In other words, the members of the Security Council—on behalf of the broad membership of the organization—would essentially use the organization as an instrument for acting at the global level. There would be far fewer unilateral uses of force than were seen during the cold war period. Force would be undertaken either by the organization itself, or perhaps more likely, through states or regional organizations to whom the United Nations had given its imprimatur. In essence, it is indeed possible that the organization could actually establish something akin to a collective security system. In such a system, states would take the prohibition on the recourse to force seriously and, through the authorization of the Security Council, would unite to take collective action against aggressors.

Second, with an increasing concern on the part of states to address multiple global resource issues, it is possible that other international organizations will be empowered to adopt binding decisions on the subject matter that they address. An example of this empowerment can be found in the International Sea-Bed Authority. This organization was established by the 1982 Convention on the Law of the Sea, which entered into force in 1994. Under the provisions of the Convention, the International Sea-Bed Authority can adopt decisions that are binding on all members of the Convention irrespective of whether they support the particular decision at the time.[6] As noted in chapter 3, certain organs of the European Union have similar powers, but the International Sea-Bed Authority is quite different. It is an organization whose decisions would affect a *global* commons. Its authority would not be limited to a particular region of the world; it would have an impact on all states and the global economy. Building upon this type of organization, it is likely that proposals will be made to empower in similar fashion organizations dealing with a host of other global commons problems. Environmental issues, such as global warming, the depletion of the ozone layer, dessertification, and deforestation seem logical issues for such an organization. At the 1992 Rio Conference, several proposals were presented to empower certain organizations to take action to regulate these and other issues. Even though many of these efforts ultimately proved unsuccessful, they indicate the willingness of many states to move in this direction. Undoubtedly, similar proposals will be presented at future conferences. If world public opinion solidifies around a desire to formally address these kinds of global resource issues, it is indeed possible that states may create more organizations that will be able to adopt resolutions that are binding upon the members of the organization.

It is even conceivable that these types of organizations may have judicial arms to resolve disputes relating to the subject matter of the organization. The Law of the Sea Convention, for example, establishes several adjudicatory and arbitral bodies to address disputes under the Convention. Under certain conditions, these bodies possess compulsory jurisdiction and the authority to issue binding decisions.[7] Other organizations could follow suit and establish similar judicial entities.

[margin note: — more toward centralization]

If these two developments toward centralization continue into the future, they could have critical implications for the nature of international law. In chapter 2, it was argued that international law at present is almost exclusively created by states. But with greater centralization, it is conceivable that something closer to true "legislation" may come to exist. With the Security Council playing a larger role in conflict management, it is possible that that body may adopt binding resolutions not only to deal with specific conflicts but also for more general purposes. In other words, alongside resolutions dealing with fighting in the Balkans or terrorism in the Middle East, the Council may adopt resolutions that set general rules for defining aggression or criteria for permitting humanitarian intervention. If this were to occur, the Security Council would actually be creating legal rules of a "legislative nature." It would not merely be addressing particular cases. In a similar vein, it is possible that the growing variety of international organizations dealing with the global commons may also adopt binding resolutions at an ever-increasing rate. If virtually all states in the international system were to join these organizations, these bodies would, in effect, also be promulgating something akin to "international legislation."

[margin note: Says Sec. Coun. will pave way + ease tensions — not only toward own interests]

2 bodies for creating law

Sec. council make laws w/ extern international resul. & States will w/ S.W.

If this projection were to prove accurate, the law-creating process would be fundamentally different than it is at present. States would still be creating international legal rules through custom and convention. But there would also be certain centralized bodies that would be empowered to create law. When a scholar or decision maker sought to determine the existence of a rule of law, he or she would also have to consult the records of certain international organizations in addition to authoritative state practice.

But is such a trend likely? Will such centralization take place within the foreseeable future? Given the recent activation of the United Nations Security Council, it seems likely that that body will indeed continue to remain a vital force, frequently passing binding resolutions with real substance. At present, however, the Council's decisions seem to be strictly limited to the particulars of individual conflicts. The Council has not adopted broad "guidelines" for dealing in general with matters under its jurisdiction. In light of a good deal of skepticism about the organization—especially skepticism coming from the permanent members of the Security Council—it seems unlikely that the Council will become a new source of "legislation" in any real sense of the word.

But what about other multilateral organizations? Perhaps they would be able to enact resolutions that will be "legislative" in nature. Here I believe that it is possible that such organizations may exercise such "legislative" power in the future, but I believe this is still a long way away. Take, for example, the International Sea-Bed Authority. Even though the Law of the Sea Convention has entered into force and the president of the United States has submitted the treaty to the Senate for advice and consent, the United States is still not a party to the Convention. There can be nothing resembling "international legislation" unless virtually all states—including those most important states—are parties. Similarly, in other issue areas, such as the environment, there are few conventions to which all these states are all members. As a consequence, while global organizations may continue to be more active, it seems that in the foreseeable future, there will be no real source of "centralized law-making." Scenario One appears unlikely; but what about Scenario Two?

IGO's may exercise legislative pwr in the future

Sec. Coun. & S.W. say centralized law not likely

SCENARIO TWO:
A NEOMEDIEVAL SYSTEM

In his classic 1977 book, *The Anarchical Society*, Professor Hedley Bull explores the future of the international system. One possibility that he discusses is that the current state system will be transformed into something akin to the medieval system that dominated Europe for nearly a thousand years. With the end of the cold war, the rise of intergovernmental organizations and other nonstate actors, several scholars have recently begun to reexamine the plausibility of the emergence of a "neomedieval" system.[8] If such a system were to emerge, it would have a profound impact on the nature of international legal rules. In this section, I will first examine the nature of a "neomedieval" system and then explore the implication of such a system for international legal rules and the rule-creating process. Finally, I will examine the prospects of such a system developing.

What is "neomedievalism"? In an extremely provocative statement for its time, Professor Bull submits that "it is conceivable that the sovereign states might disappear and be replaced not by a world government but by a modern and secular equivalent of the kind of universal political organisation that existed in Western Christendom in the Middle Ages."[9] "In that system," explains Bull, "no ruler or state was sovereign in the sense of being supreme over a given territory and a given segment of the Christian population; each had to share authority with vassals beneath, and with the Pope and (in Germany and Italy) the Holy Roman Emperor above."[10] While "it might . . . seem fanciful to contemplate a return to the mediaeval model," avers Bull, "it is not fanciful to imagine that there might develop a modern and secular counterpart of it that embodies its central characteristic: a system of overlapping authority and multiple loyalty."[11] Such a system, if it were to develop, would be a fundamentally different international political system. As Professors Bruce Cronin and Joseph Lepgold note, a neomedieval system would be one "defined by actors of increased *diversity* and *heterogeneity* and characterized by overlapping international authorities and conflicting loyalties."[12] In such a system, there may be territorial states, but there would be other actors as well. Individuals in this system would owe loyalty to a variety of different authorities. These might include substate actors (like autonomous ethnic communities, such as the Bosnian Serbs or the Palestinians), suprastate actors (like integrated regional organizations, such as the European Union), transnational organizations (such as the Catholic Church), intergovernmental organizations of various varieties (such as the United Nations), nongovernmental organizations (such as Amnesty International), trans-state associations (such as the Alpine-Adria Working Group), transnational corporations (such as Shell Oil or IBM), and so on. These and other nonstate actors would not merely be adjuncts of states but would have real power and command real loyalty.[13]

In 1977, Bull noted five trends that some have suggested as *possibly* leading to the development of "a secular reincarnation of the system of overlapping or segmented authority that characterised mediaeval Christendom."[14] These were regional integration of states, the disintegration of states, the restoration of private international violence, transnational organizations, and the technological unification of the world. Taking these trends as a point of departure, the rough contours of a neomedieval system can be set forth.

First, Bull observes the trend toward regional integration. At the time of his writing, the only real example was the European Community, although he notes the influence of the European effort on similar ventures in Africa, Latin America, and Asia. Bull explains that, "it is possible that the process of integration might arrive at the stage where, while one could not speak of a European state, there was real doubt both in theory and in reality as to whether sovereignty lay with the national governments or with the organs of the 'community.'"[15] Since the time this sentence was written, the European Community—now the European Union—has grown both in numbers and in terms of the authority of its organs. It has not become merely a large state, which, as Bull notes, would not be a fundamental challenge to the state system, but has created an arrangement in which certain loyalties are owed to the Union and certain authority really does rest in the organs of the Union. Indeed, as Ole Waever has recently observed, changes in Europe "create a pressure in the direction of a complexity that could be labelled neomedieval."[16] Waever explains that "the presently emerging political structures can be seen as 'neomedieval' in the sense that

West European political organization no longer fits into the format of territorial sovereignty and exclusivity."[17] "The nation-states," he continues, "are not sovereign, but nor is the EU a sovereign state."[18]

Second, Bull notes that the disintegration of states could also contribute to the development of a neomedieval structure. This would not come about if secessionist movements lead to the creation of new states, but rather if ethnic and other groups currently within states became semi-autonomous actors in the system of a fundamentally new nature. They would not be states, but they would have authority over individuals and the right to interact with other international actors. As Bull explains, "if these new units were to advance far enough towards sovereign statehood both in terms of accepted doctrine and in terms of their command of force and human loyalties, and yet at the same time were to stop short of claiming that same sovereignty for themselves, the situation might arise in which the institution of sovereignty itself might go into decline."[19]

When Bull wrote, state disintegration had not created these kinds of actors. After over twenty years, however, there are now a number of actors in the international system that are similar to the units of which Bull spoke. The disintegration of Yugoslavia, for example, has produced several states in the traditional sense, but it has also produced nonstate actors that have authority and command loyalty—the Bosnian Serbs or the Croatian Serbs. These groups have political structures, and political leaders, but are not states. They are, however, important actors in the international arena. In a similar vein, the Palestinian entity that has been established in the Middle East is an important nonstate actor. It has certain territorial control, a governing structure, the ability to enter into international agreements, and other rights. But again, it is not at present a state.

The third trend that Bull discusses is what he calls the restoration of private international violence. By this he means the growing presence of groups that use force against states and other international actors and claim the right to engage in such uses of force. The existence of such groups could, according to Bull, challenge one of the most basic features of the state system: "the state's monopoly of legitimate international violence."[20] When Bull was making these observations, there were a great number of terrorist groups and other political groups using force in the international system. "What is more impressive than the fact that international violence is resorted to by these non-state groups," explains Bull, "is the fact that their claim of the right to do so is accepted as legitimate by a substantial proportion of international society."[21] As an example of this legitimacy, one might cite the 1974 United Nations General Assembly "Definition of Aggression." Article 7 of this Resolution provides that

> nothing in this Definition . . . could in any way prejudice the right to self-determination, freedom and independence, as derived from the [United Nations] Charter, of peoples forcibly deprived of the right referred to in the Declaration on Principles of International Law concerning Friendly Relations and Co-operation among States in accordance with the Charter of the United Nations, particular peoples under colonial and racist regimes or other forms of alien domination; *nor the right of these people to struggle to that end and to seek and receive support*, in accordance with the principles of the Charter and in conformity with the above mentioned Declaration.[22]

Even though this Resolution is a nonbinding General Assembly Resolution, it does seem to confer a certain legitimacy to force used by self-determination movements seeking to fight alien, racist, and colonial regimes.

In the international system today, there does seem to be a dramatic increase in "private violence." In the wake of the violence in the Middle East and Latin America, the bombings of the American embassies in Kenya and Tanzania, terrorist groups seem active as ever. Islamic Jihad, the Abu Nidal group, and a host of other terrorist organizations have been active players in international politics. While some terrorist groups may not have been accorded international legitimacy, other nonstate actors engaged in violence—such as the Bosnian Serbs—do seem to have been granted certain legitimacy. That is, they have been seen as actors that have rights to negotiate and enter into international agreements. Private violence has also manifested itself in the behavior of a variety of other actors. International criminal organzations have developed global networks and their own norms for using force. Moreover, as will be noted later, private security and policing forces have begun to play an increasingly greater role in world affairs.

A fourth trend that Bull suggests could be leading to a change in the international system is the growing number of what he calls "transnational organisations." He explains that "this is the organisation which operates across international boundaries, sometimes on a global scale, which seeks as far as possible to disregard these boundaries, and which serves to establish links between different national societies, or sections of these societies."[23] Within this category, Bull includes multinational corporations, political movements, nongovernmental organizations, religious organizations, and even "intergovernmental agencies that operate across frontiers, such as the World Bank."[24] Bull explains that "it is often argued that these transnational organisations, or some of them, because they bypass the states system and contribute directly to the knitting together of the global society or the global economy, are bringing about the states system's demise."[25]

As with the previous trends noted by Bull, there has been a proliferation of these kinds of arrangements over the past several decades. Indeed, groups such as Amnesty International, Greenpeace, and the Catholic Church have been especially active in world politics. They have interacted with states on important political issues and have obtained the loyalty of many people throughout the world. Moreover, transnational corporations (TNCs) have increasingly been playing a remarkable role in international politics. Professor Susan Strange argues that "we can conclude that while TNCs do not take over from the governments of states, they have certainly encroached on their domains of power."[26] "They are," she explains, "increasingly exercizing a parallel authority alongside governments in matters of economic management affecting the location of industry and investment, the direction of technological innovation, the management of labour relations and the fiscal extraction of surplus value."[27]

The fifth and final trend that Bull presents is the technological unification of the world. He explains that some individuals would argue "that the demise of the states system is taking place as a consequence of the technological unification of the world—of which the multinational corporations and the non-state groups which conduct international violence are only particular expressions, and which is bound to lead to the politics of 'spaceship earth' or of the 'global village' in which the states system is only a part."[28]

While Bull has strong reservations about any kind of real "unification" coming about, it seems clear that technology can forge new loyalties and identities that can provide serious challenges to the existing state system. Epistemic communities can be strengthened; people can come in contact with others at the touch of a button. Since *The Anarchical Society* was written, technological developments have advanced exponentially. The fax machine and the Internet have begun to establish new linkages among people and groups. Moreover, electronic communication has facilitated the instant transfer of financial resources in ways that may not be easily susceptible to state control.

Before exploring the implications of these trends for international law, I want to add one more development to Bull's list. Over the past several years, substate actors in Europe have been entering into political, commercial, and economic arrangements with each other, forming a type of trans-state association.[29] In the 1980s, for example, the Alpine-Adria Working Group was established. Consisting of 16 "province-level members" from five European states, this association sought to foster cooperation on cultural, environmental, communications, transportation, and other areas. In a similar vein, cities like Lyon, France, Geneva, Switzerland, and Turin, Italy have created the so-called Alpine Diamond, a cooperative arrangement in which these cities attempt to share economic resources.[30] Needless to say, if these kinds of trans-state associations continue, they could produce tremendous inroads on the traditional roles of the state.

If these trends do, in fact, continue there could be significant changes for international legal rules. As noted in chapter 2, states are still the main actors in the international system and the primary creators of international law. Even though nonstate actors exist, and, in some cases, these nonstate actors have entered into international agreements, these actors do not enter into the process of creating general international law in an unmediated fashion. In other words, the interactions of nonstate actors with each other and with states do not produce customary international law. Only state interactions can produce custom. If, however, the state were to lose its monopoly in a neomedieval system, the most basic general principle about the nature of international law—the notion that *states* create international law through their consent—would now have to be expanded. If this were to be the case, the international law-creating process would be fundamentally changed. This change would be reflected in at least two specific developments.

neo medieval can lead to...

First, the process of creating customary international law could become much more complex. There could, in fact, be multiple levels of customary international law. At one level, there could be some rules of customary international law that were binding on all types of international actors. In those cases, instead of authoritative state practice alone producing customary legal rules, the mutual interactions of a variety of international actors—states, substate actors, "peoples," and international organizations—would constitute general customary international law. If a scholar or other observer wished to determine the existence of a rule of international law of this nature, he or she could not examine merely state practice, but would need to examine the practice of this entire panoply of actors. Thus, for example, suppose an observer wished to determine what legal rules applied to the interpretation of international agreements. In a neomedieval system, that observer would need to apply the authority-control test very differently. First, the observer would need to examine the perceptions of authority of the decision-making elites from all the different types of international actors. What do these elites in states perceive? What do those in substate actors perceive? What do those in intergovernmental organizations perceive? What do those elites in nongovernmental organizations perceive? Second, the observer would then need to examine what rules are controlling of the behavior of all international actors. What rules of interpretation are used for agreements among states? Between states and nongovernmental organizations? Between states and substate actors? Among nongovernmental organizations? Among substate actors? And, the examination would go on until all combinations had been examined. Finally, the observer could pronounce that a particular rule was binding customary international law on all actors in the system.

But at a second level, it is also possible that there could be rules of customary international law that are binding on some, but not all, international actors. There could, for example, be certain rules that apply only to the relations among states, others that apply only to the relations among intergovernmental organizations, and still others that apply to the relations between states and nongovernmental organizations. Once again, the scholar or other observer would need to apply the authority-control tests to these various kinds of interactions to determine the specific legal rules. One of the most difficult tasks for the scholar would be to determine the boundaries of the rule. To which actors does it apply?

Second, the process for determining general principles common to the domestic legal systems would also be much more complex. As noted in chapter 2, one interpretation of general principles that has widespread acceptance is that there are certain principles common to the world's domestic legal systems that can be applied to disputes among states. In a neomedieval system, this notion would need to be expanded. While there may still be certain principles common to the domestic legal systems of *states* that could be applied in certain cases, there may also be certain legal principles that are applied in the "internal" legal systems of a variety of actors that would have international applicability. A scholar might have to consult the operating rules of intergovernmental organizations, substate actors, and so on, in order to determine what these rules are and when they apply.

In sum, if the world were to move into something resembling a neomedieval structure, international law as we know it would change fundamentally. With a change in the a priori assumption that states are the sole creators of general international law, the process for creating both customary international law and general principles of law would alter significantly. The task for the scholar or anyone else would become extremely complicated, if not unmanageable. As difficult as assessing state practice may be, the task of exploring the authoritative practice of a wide variety of international actors would be exceptionally daunting.

But however daunting this task may be, if the international system is moving in this direction, scholars, government officials, and others will have little choice. But is the international system moving toward a neomedieval structure? When Hedley Bull was writing in 1977, he concluded that a neomedieval system had not yet come about. Despite the trends that he observed, he believed that the contemporary state system would continue. He noted that "if some of the trends towards a 'new mediaevalism' that have been reviewed here were to go much further, such a situation might come about, but it would be going beyond the evidence to conclude that 'groups other than the state' have made inroads on the sovereignty of states that the states system is now giving away to this alternative."[31] But, as noted above, some of the trends Bull observed *have gone further*. The disintegration of states has created a variety of nonstate actors, such as the Bosnian Serbs. Regional integration in Europe has given rise to multiple authorities in the European community. Private violence in the form of numerous terrorist and liberation organizations has empowered certain nonstate actors in the system. Many transnational organizations—like the Catholic Church—are playing increasingly important roles. And the Internet has brought about a greater unification of peoples than Bull probably imagined. Does this mean that neomedievalism is nearly upon us? Will the state system as it is currently constituted be replaced by a fundamentally different paradigm for international relations?

Despite the trends noted above, there are several developments that suggest that the contemporary state system will persist. First, and perhaps ironically, the resurgence of the United Nations suggests the continuing primacy of states as actors. As the cold war was coming to an end, the United Nations, as noted earlier, was gaining strength. It played an unprecedented role in the Gulf War and continues to be involved in peace operations throughout the world to an extent previously unknown. Although far from completely successful, it is now a major player in world politics. But despite the supranational appearance of the United Nations, it remains fundamentally an organization of *states*. When the "United Nations" acts, it is the members of the organization who are acting.[32] Moreover, one of the major roles of the organization is to confer legitimacy upon states and, by implication, the state system itself. Admission to the United Nations is a crucial element in gaining membership into the international community. As the Soviet Union and Yugoslavia were breaking up, an important factor in the legitimization of these new units was their admission to the United Nations. Accordingly, as the United Nations continues to act as an organization of states and confers legitimacy upon states, it reaffirms the state system itself.

Second, many of the trends toward neomedievalism have persisted in the past without fundamentally altering the nature of the state system. Bull himself notes that the trends he describes "are awkward facts for the classical theory of world politics as simply the relations between states."[33] But, he continues, "that theory . . . has always had to contend with the existence of anomalies and irregularities."[34] After noting a number of these historical challenges, he explains that "the classical theory has held sway not because it can account for all the complexity of universal politics, but because it has provided a truer guide to it than alternative visions."[35] "A time may come," Bull admits, "when the anomalies and irregularities are so glaring that an alternative theory, better able to take account of these realities, will come to dominate the field."[36] But, he concludes, "there is no clear evidence that in the next few decades the states system is likely to give place to any of the alternatives to it that have been nominated."[37]

he believes neomedieval

Yet notwithstanding these two arguments in support of the continuation of the current state system, I believe that developments seem to be pointing toward the emergence of a neomedieval system. First, while it is true that the United Nations continues to play a critical role in affirming states, it is also playing an increasing role in acknowledging the status of nonstate actors. Even in the face of Western opposition some years ago, the United Nations and a number of affiliated agencies granted observer status to groups such as the Palestine Liberation Organization[38] and the South West African Peoples Organization.[39] Indeed, in July of 1998, the United Nations General Assembly granted "additional rights" to the Palestine delegate, including the "right to participate in the general debate of the Assembly, to speak under agenda items other than Palestinian and Middle East issues at any meeting of the plenary, and to exercise the right of reply."[40] In addition, the United Nations has continued to affirm the rights of numerous ethnic groups, such as the Kurds and the Shiite's in Iraq. It has also dealt with groups like the Bosnian Serbs and Croatian Serbs, giving credence to their position as actors in international politics. Moreover, the very existence of the United Nations and the great host of other intergovernmental organizations supports a neomedieval understanding of the world. This is especially true as these organizations begin to be perceived not merely as representatives of states, but as another type of "independent" actor in the system.

All focuses on UN + what it has done. Flaw?

Second, I believe that these trends have progressed beyond the point Bull observed, and that they will continue to intensify in the immediate future. Why? I would cite three factors.

First, the cold war is over. During the period of Western colonization, states were created in many areas where there had been no
Westphalian tradition of the sovereign state. As Professors Cronin and
Lepgold observe, "during the Cold War, it was in the interests of the
superpowers and the other great powers to sustain these state structures, but this concern quickly disappeared after the Cold War's demise."[41] "The rapidity of disintegration in such countries as Somalia, Rwanda, and Liberia," they explain, "attests to the fragility of
the state, at least in Africa."[42] With many such fragile states, and the
unwillingness of great powers to intervene purely to maintain these
structures, the possibility of further disintegration seems high.

Second, states are becoming increasingly incapable of providing for
the needs of their citizens as those citizens keep asking more and more
from their states. As Cronin and Lepgold note, "populations are ex-
pecting and demanding more from the state in almost every area, from
economic prosperity to the provision of services."[43] "Since the mid
twentieth century," they continue, "the nation-state has been required
to undertake organizational tasks on a scale far greater than anything
it had previously attempted."[44] They explain that "increased demands
have been placed upon states by technological changes, by the inter-
nationalization of trade and finance, and by the growth of transnational
interactions among sub-state and non-state actors."[45] With these ris-
ing expectations on the part of populations and the inability of states
to perform, "individuals and communities have . . . begun to look elsewhere to fill these needs."[46] They have looked to trans-state associations, international organizations, substate arrangements, and so forth.
Several examples can be cited.

One striking example of communities looking to other entities
to fulfill needs has been "the rapid rise in private security and policing throughout the advanced industrial world."[47] In the United States,
for example, there are numerous private police forces for certain
exclusive communities, commercial security operations for corporations, community security patrols, and even college and university
police forces. As Cronin and Lepgold note, "by most definitions,
safety is the single most important function of state authority."[48] Yet,
"if other institutions and authorities continue to take on the role of

providing it, the state will lose its monopoly on the legitimate use of violence within territorial borders."[49] When this happens, states will no longer be able to maintain their primacy in the structure of the international system.

A second—and related—indicator of the growing inability of states to meet the needs of their people is the increased use of private military forces or "mercenaries" by states themselves. As Professor Herbert Howe contended in 1998, "the growth of private military and police capability is staggering, especially in Eastern Europe, wealthy Middle Eastern states and threatened African states."[50] Employing many former state military officers and enlisted personnel, organizations such as Military Professional Resources, Incorporated (MPRI) and Executive Outcomes have been playing critical roles. MPRI, for example, "has 182 former U.S. Special Forces personnel training and equipping the Bosnia Federation's military force."[51] "Executive Outcomes," to take another example, "fielded about 600 combat soldiers in Angola and 300 men in Sierra Leone to help defeat insurgencies."[52] Moreover, "EO's air capabilities, including MI-8, 17 and 24 helicopters and MiG 23 fighters, supported these soldiers."[53] This use of private military forces by states in international conflict has implications similar to the privatization of policing within states. It reflects an inability of states to perform what had been perceived to be a core function of the state—the defense of the realm.[54]

Finally, many transnational corporations are providing needed goods and services to individuals that states formerly provided. A great variety of examples could be cited. Two examples that Professor Strange gives are accounting firms and insurance companies. As she explains, "both were originally adjuncts of state authority, governed by institutions to whom national governments delegated a special kind of functional power necessary to a capitalist system of accumulation and production."[55] Over time, however, both types of companies "came increasingly to operate across frontiers, time zones and currency areas."[56] With this development, "these professions are able to operate more independently of state authority, yet with a great impact on the lives and options open to others."[57] Here again, we see nonstate entities responding to needs in the international system. They, like many other nonstate actors discussed above, serve as competing authorities and represent another important indication of the weakening of the state system.

Third, another factor pointing toward the emergence of a neo-medieval system is evidence that states may already be losing some significant degree of control over the law-making process. This can be seen in the growing activities of international criminal organizations. These organizations—"mafias"[58] as Professor Susan Strange labels them—began as domestic organizations but have become transnational over time.[59] According to Strange, there is presently a "network of links being forged between organised crime in different parts of the world."[60] In addition to "the Sicilian and American Cosa Nostras," she reports that now "there are half a dozen other major transnational criminal organisations, most of them connected to the Cosa Nostra by informal agreements and shared interests."[61] Not suprisingly, "the newcomers to the global network are the numerous mafias that have grown up inside the former Soviet Union."[62] Indeed, Strange notes that "one estimate cited in 1995 by the chief prosecutor of Florence suggested that organised criminal groups in Russia then controlled 35 per cent of the commercial banks, 40 per cent of the former State-owned industry, 35 per cent of the private enterprise—and as much as 60 per cent of commerce and 80 per cent of joint ventures with foreign firms."[63]

These various criminal organizations are increasingly asserting a great deal of control over the international political economy and usurping state authority. Much of this usurpation has come about through the tacit consent of states themselves. As Professor Strange explains, "ever since the Westphalian treaty in Europe, it has been held that the determination of what was and what is not 'the wrong side of the law' lay in the last resort with the governments of territorial states."[64] But "in recent years," she explains, "the majority of such governments have taken two intrinsically conflicting decisions—on the possession and sale of stupefying or hallucinatory drugs, and on financial transactions through the banking system involving clean and dirty money."[65] While the first area—possessing and selling drugs—"has been declared the wrong side of the law," "the second has been tacitly admitted as being on the right side, inasmuch as only the most feeble attempts have been used to make the banks responsible, as criminal accessories, to the laundering of money acquired by criminal activities—whether bribes, robbery or illegal trafficking."[66] And, as Strange argues, "the contradiction between the two decisions, that selling drugs is illegal but handling the financial proceeds of the trade is not, is putting the entire system of state authority at risk."[67]

If Strange is correct in her assessment, this development does indeed represent a profound challenge to the state system as we know it. At the most basic level, the growing activity of transnational criminal organizations is yet another example of nonstate actors providing goods and services to individuals that the state is unable—or in this case, unwilling—to provide. But at a deeper level, the turn of events to which Strange points illustrates an even greater challenge to the Westphalian system—the inability of states to determine legal rules in certain circumstances. States, she argues, deem the drug trade (and certain other activities) to be illegal and take appropriate action to enforce these laws. Moreover, states contend that the financial transactions associated with these activities are also "illegal." But, claims Strange, states do not really takes this latter claim relating to financial transactions seriously. In their practice, states are essentially turning a blind eye to these types of financial operations. All this suggests that states may be allowing certain transnational actors to determine what are genuinely authoritative and controlling rules. While states may seem to set rules about financial transactions, these rules appear to be lacking in real authority and actual control. If this is indeed the case, this may be one critical area where nonstate actors—in fine neomedieval fashion—are already participating in the law-creating process in a more direct manner.

CONCLUSION

These recent developments suggest that the international system is in a period of profound transformation. Despite the persistence of the Westphalian state system for the past three hundred and fifty years, I believe the future of that system lies in the balance. While the current system is still properly characterized as a "state system," a host of trends point to the emergence of a very different kind of international system, a neomedieval system. In such a system, states would only be one actor among many. The loyalities of individuals would be divided among those various actors. There is no reason to believe that legal rules will be absent from such a system. But it seems clear that the process of creating legal rules will be fundamentally altered. General international law will come about through the many interactions of the multiple international actors. And the task for the scholar or other observer will become much more difficult. How long it will be before such a neomedieval system is "in place" is impossible to predict. Given the current trajacetory of the developments discussed above, however, it does not seem to be unreasonable to expect the emergence of such a system in the early part of the twenty-first century.

NOTES

1. These scenarios will be presented against the background of the current state system. It is of course possible that the current system will persist into the future. It may remain a state-based, anarchic arrangement. If this were to prove to be the case, the international legal system would also remain essentially the same. There might be changes in the specific substantive legal rules, but the process through which legal rules are created by state consent would not change in any significant fashion.

2. Hedley Bull, *The Anarchical Society* 254 (1977).

3. I have examined this literature in greater depth in Anthony Clark Arend, The United Nations and the New World Order, 81 *Georgetown L. J.* (1993).

4. For a discussion of the actions against Iraq, see Anthony Clark Arend & Robert J. Beck, *International Law and the Use of Force: Beyond the UN Charter Paradigm* 53–55 (1993). See also Paul Lewis, UN Gives Iraq Until Jan. 15 to Retreat or Face Force: Hussein Says He Will Fight, *New York Times*, Nov. 30, 1990, A1, col. 6; John M. Goshko, UN Authorizes Use of Force Against Iraq, *Washington Post*, Nov. 30, 1990 A1, col. 4.

5. This information is taken from the United Nations Website: http://www.org/Depts/dpko/troop/a-troop.htm. As of the end of 1995, it was reported that the United Nations was sponsoring 15 peace operations, involving more than 30,000 participants. Boutros Boutros-Ghali, *Confronting New Challenges: Annual Report of the Work of the Organization* 221 (1995).

6. The 1982 Convention gives certain rule-making powers to both the Assembly and the Council of the International Sea-Bed Authority. See official text of the United Nations Convention on the Law of the Sea, arts. 156–165.

7. See Law of the Sea Convention, arts. 286–299.

8. Some scholars that have begun exploring this idea are Professors Thomas M. Franck, and Bruce Cronin and Joseph Lepgold. See Bruce Cronin and Joseph Lepgold, A New Medievalism? Conflicting International Authorities and Competing Localities in the Twenty-First Century, unpublished paper presented at the conference on "The Changing Nature of Sovereignty in the New World Order," Center for International Affairs, Harvard University, April 1995; Thomas M. Franck, "Tribe, Nation, World: Self-Identification in the Evolving World Community," William V. O'Brien Lecture in International Law and Morality, Georgetown University, Sept. 22, 1995.

9. Hedley Bull, *The Anarchical Society*, at 254.

10. Id.

11. Id.

12. Bruce Cronin and Joseph Lepgold, A New Medievalism? at 5.

13. For Bull, a neomedieval system can develop only if sovereignty ceases to be the ordering principle of the international system. He explains that

the mere existence in world politics of actors other than the state, however, does not provide any indication of a trend toward a new mediaevalism. The crucial question is whether the inroads being made by these "other associations" (to use the mediaevalists' expression) on the sovereignty or supremacy of the state over its territory and citizens is such as to make that supremacy unreal, and to deprive the concept of sovereignty of its utility and viability.

Hedley Bull, *The Anarchical Society*, at 264.

14. Id.

15. Id. at 266.

16. Ole Waever, Imperial Metaphors: Emerging European Analogies to Pre-Nation-State Imperial Systems, in Ola Tunander, Pavel Baev & Victoria Ingrid Einagel, eds. *Geopolitics in Post-Wall Europe* 57, 86 (1997).

17. Id.

18. Id.

19. Hedley Bull, *The Anarchical Society*, at 267.

20. Id. at 268.

21. Id. at 268–269.

22. Definition of Aggression Resolution, G.A. Res. 3314, UN G.A.O.R., 29th Sess., Supp. 31, UN Doc. a/9631, at 141 (1974) (emphasis added). See Anthony Clark Arend & Robert J. Beck, *International Law and the Use of Force*, at 40–42, for a discussion of the implications of this Resolution.

23. Hedley Bull, *The Anarchical Society*, at 270.

24. Id.

25. Id. at 271.

26. Susan Strange, *The Retreat of the State: The Diffusion of Power in the World Economy* 65 (1996).

27. Id.

28. Hedley Bull, *The Anarchical Society*, at 273.

29. I am grateful to Lt. Col. Chris A. Pilecki (USA) for mentioning this development to me. This section draws upon a jointly authored article that is in process.

30. See William Drozdiak, Regions on the Rise, *Washington Post*, Oct. 22, 1995.

31. Hedley Bull, *The Anarchical Society*, at 275.

32. This is a point that Professor Inis L. Claude, Jr. has consistently made over the years.

33. Hedley Bull, *The Anarchical Society*, at 274.

34. Id.

35. Id. at 275.

36. Id.

37. Id.

38. See G.A. Res. 3237 (XXIX) G.A.O.R., 29th Sess., Supp. 31, at 4 (1974).

39. See G.A. Res. 3280 (XXIX) G.A.O.R., 29th Sess., Supp. 31, at 5 (1974); G.A.Res. 31/30, (XXXI) G.A.O.R., 31st Sess., Supp. 39, at 118 (1976).

40. United Nations Press Release, GA/9427, <http://www.un.org/plweb-cgi/iopcode.p>

41. Bruce Cronin and Joseph Lepgold, A New Medievalism? at 26.

42. Id. at 26–27.

43. Id. at 19.

44. Id.

45. Id. at 20.

46. Id. at 19.

47. Id at 33. Cronin and Lepgold cite an unpublished manuscript by Professor Janice Thompson entitled "The Privatization of Policing: Implications for State Sovereignty."

48. Id.

49. Id.

50. Herbert M. Howe, Global Order and the Privatization of Security, 22 *Fletcher Forum of World Affairs* 1, 2 (1998).

51. Id.

52. Id. at 3.

53. Id.

54. Id. at 1.
55. Susan Strange, *The Retreat of the State*, at 92.
56. Id.
57. Id.
58. Id. at 110–121.
59. Id. at 111–112.
60. Id. at 111.
61. Id.
62. Id. at 112.
63. Id. (reference in text is to *La Republica*, 28 January 1995).
64. Id. at 118.
65. Id. at 118–119.
66. Id. at 119.
67. Id.

SIX

LEGAL RULES AND INTERNATIONAL SOCIETY

In the introduction to this book, I set forth several reasons for undertaking a fresh examination of international legal rules. First, I noted the need to rehabilitate the study of international law within the discipline of international relations. Second, I cited the need to return legal scholarship to a closer examination of empirical data—state practice. Finally, I mentioned the need to reexamine the nature of international legal rules in the wake of changes in the international system.

In the light of these propositions, this book has sought to accomplish four major tasks. First, it has endeavored to demonstrate that international legal rules are distinctive—they are different from other types of rules in international politics. Second, this work has developed a new methodology for examining state practice to determine the existence of international legal rules. Based on the premise that legal rules are created through the consent of states, I have sought to provide a methodology that both scholars and practitioners can use to determine whether a putative rule is, in fact, a *legal* rule. Third, using a constructivist approach, this book has argued that legal rules play a critical role in contemporary international politics. Any student of international relations must, I believe, understand the nature and operation of international legal rules in order to have an accurate understanding of how the international system works. Fourth, this book has explored recent trends in international politics that suggest that the structure of the system may be undergoing fundamental change. In particular, I have attempted to demonstrate that the contemporary state system is moving in the direction of a neomedieval arrangement—a system with a diversity of actors and overlapping loyalties. Such a development would have profound implications for the manner in which international legal rules are created.

The nature of this examination of legal rules in international politics points, I believe, to two further conclusions. The first might be called a "substantive" conclusion; the second could perhaps be termed a "methodological" conclusion. The substantive conclusion is that the existence of international legal rules supports, if not proves, that there is, at least at some level, an "international society." The methodological conclusion is that interdisciplinary cooperation must progress if scholars and public officials are to be able to comprehend international relations, especially as the system undergoes change. In the final chapter of this book, I will not rehash the substance of previous chapters, but I would like to explore these two additional conclusions.

INTERNATIONAL SOCIETY

The title of this work is *Legal Rules and International Society*. And perhaps by now a reader may be wondering whether something more should have been said about "international society." It is true that in chapter 4 I use constructivism, which amounts to a sociological approach to understanding international legal rules. Implicit in that approach, I would submit, is the notion of an international society. But I believe that I need to be more explicit at this point. In particular, I would like to do three things. First, I will attempt to define international society. Second, I will examine how legal rules support the existence of a "society of states" in the current international system. And third, I will explore how new developments are pointing toward the emergence of a very different kind of international society.

International Society

As noted in previous chapters, the late Professor Hedley Bull wrote of the existence of an "anarchical society." To some commentators, this phrase may have seem contradictory. How can there be a society in "anarchy"? But to Bull and others this was not a contradiction, the international system was anarchic because there was "no common power," but it was still a society because there were certain shared values among participants. For Bull, an international society existed "when a group of states, conscious of certain common interests and common values, form a society in the sense that they conceive themselves to be bound by a common set of rules in their relations with one another, and share in the working of common institutions."[1] He explains that "if states today form an international society . . . this is because, recognising certain common interests and perhaps some common values, they regard themselves bound by certain rules in their dealings with one another, such as that they should respect one another's claims to independence, that they should honour agreements into which they enter, and that they should be subject to certain limitations in exercising force against one another."[2] "At the same time," he continues, "they cooperate in the working of institutions such as the forms of procedures of international law, the machinery of diplomacy and general international organisation, and the customs and conventions of war."[3] Common interests, common values, common rules, and common institutions can exist, even in the absence of any true system of centralized government. If they do, it can be said that there is an international society.[4]

A Society of States?

In the light of Bull's definition of international society, does such a thing exist in the contemporary international system? Can we say that there is some kind of society at the global level? This book has, I believe, demonstrated that there is an international society, rudimentary perhaps, but a society nonetheless.

This work has sought to establish that there are distinctive legal rules that regulate the behavior of international actors. These rules are created through the consent of states in a process that is accepted by these states. Through the conclusion of treaties, the development of custom, and the acceptance of general principles of law, states create rules that are both authoritative and controlling. They create international law. This fact points, I would submit, to the reality of international society. The very existence of international legal rules means that there are certain common interests, common values, common rules, and common institutions. First, legal rules exist precisely because states have certain common interests to regulate. Whether it is diplomatic intercourse, the use of oceans resources, the protection of the environment, the delimitation of state jurisdiction, the use of outer space, or whatever area of the law one may choose, these rules have developed because there was at least some degree of common interest on the part of states. States wanted to regulate these issues in some common way. This assertion should not, of course, be exaggerated to the point of assuming that states have nothing but common interests or that these common interests are greater than they are. But to the extent that there are any legal rules, there are areas of common interest. Second, the existence of legal rules reflects certain common values. At the highest level of abstraction, international legal rules indicate a desire on the part of all members of the international system for some modicum of order. To establish legal rules is to value order. The rules seek to provide regularity of behavior and predictability. Indeed, one of the most important first principles about the nature of the international legal system, *pacta sunt servanda*, illustrates a shared value in order. Legal rules also embody a variety of more specific shared values—such as the notion that states are sovereign, that they are the constitutive actors for legal rules, and so on. Third, international legal rules are by definition a type of rule that plays a role on the global plane. Despite what a hyperrealist might assert, there are legal rules that regulate the behavior of states and other actors in the international system. The international system may be anarchic in the formal sense, but it is not a Hobbesian state of war of all against all. Rules exist. Finally, the presence of legal rules demonstrates the existence of common institutions. Using the term "institution" in the broadest sense, there is a common "international legal institution." That is, there is a regular process for creating legal rules that has received universal acceptance.

While states may quibble about whether a particular putative rule is law, they would not quibble about the existence of the legal institution itself.

In short, the presence of an international legal system indicates that there is some form of international society. It may not be as well developed a society as found within states, but it still possesses certain common interests, values, rules, and institutions. There is a society of states.

The Future of the Society of States

But even as the contemporary international legal system demonstrates the existence of a society of states, the numerous trends discussed earlier point to changes in the nature of this society. If, as submitted in chapter 5, the state system is being transformed into a neomedieval system, a different kind of society may be emerging. It would no longer be a society of states in the strict sense due to the increased role of nonstate actors. But what kind of society would it be?

One possibility is that the society of states is being replaced by what might be called a "society of humankind."[5] In such a society, existing state boundaries would be of much less significance. Individuals from all parts of the world would perceive themselves to be part of a world society in which common interests, common values, common rules, and common institutions existed globally. In such a system, states might play the same role that provinces or federal states do in existing national societies. They may be political units that exercise certain governmental functions, but not sovereign entities that stand in the way of a larger society. In this type of society, there would not be international law as currently understood, but some form of "world law," with individual human beings as the primary entities possessing legal personality.

While such a society of humankind may exist in a spiritual sense, the likelihood of the emergence of such a society in a political sense seems remote. Even though it could be claimed that individuals are playing an increasingly greater role in the international legal system, the predominant form of international interaction remains associational. In other words, it is not primarily persons who engage in international relations but associations composed of people—states, international organizations, trans-state associations, substate actors, and the like. Even if the world is moving toward a neomedieval structure, individuals will still be interacting in this associational manner. It could only be in the very distant future that a political society of humankind could emerge. The international arena seems a very long way from any real system of world law and world governance in which people and not associations are the primary actors.

Given the slim prospects that a society of humankind will emerge any time soon, what other form might international society take? As the international system continues to change, I believe that what we may begin to observe is the development of a "society of associations." As noted previously, a neomedieval system would be composed of a variety of international actors. States may exist, but they would exist alongside several different types of nonstate actors. As common interests, common values, common rules, and common institutions would begin to develop *among* these different types of associations, a society would develop among them.

Such a society of associations would be "messy." The units would be dissimilar. We are extremely accustomed to thinking of societies composed of like entities—a society of people or a society of states. Moreover, as noted in the previous chapter, the common legal rules for such a system could be much more difficult to determine than those for a system of states. But assuming the variety of actors continues to increase and these actors continue to play a direct role in world politics, this type of international society seems likely to emerge.

THE NEED FOR INTERDISCIPLINARY COLLABORATION

One of the major purposes of this book has been to provide an exploration of international legal rules that is useful to both international legal scholars and international relations theorists. As noted in the introduction, despite the estrangement that has existed for decades between the two disciplines, there is now a great deal of scholarly interest in collaborative efforts.[6] Students of both international law and international relations are seeking new ways to grasp an understanding of each other's approach to rules. Articles are being written; conferences are being held. While there are undoubtedly many reasons for this interaction to continue, this book points to the need for such interdisciplinary work to continue for at least two specific reasons. First, interdisciplinary research is necessary in order to explore more closely the role of international legal rules in international politics. Second, the two disciplines must work closely together in order to understand the dramatic changes that may be occurring in the international system. Let me elaborate briefly on these two reasons.

The Role of International Legal Rules in International Politics

In chapter 4, I attempted to examine the role that legal rules play in contemporary international relations. Using a constructivist approach, I submitted that legal rules may actually alter the identity and thus the interests of the actors in the system. While I gave several examples of this phenomenon in the context of the chapter, there has been virtually no other empirical exploration of this process. Yet I believe that legal rules provide an excellent laboratory for the examination of how a certain structure can change the identity of actors. But for such research to go forward, there needs to be close collaboration between both international relations scholars and international legal scholars. Many international relations scholars, I would submit, are not really aware of specific legal rules and the role that they can play in changing identity. Similarly, most legal scholars are probably not even conscious of the "identity issue" that international relations theorists have raised. In a collaboration, legal scholars can help identify the nature of the legal rules or, if you will, the legal regime that exists, and international relations scholars can present the theoretical issues at stake. Together they can assess the changes in identity that may be taking place. Such collaboration would go a long way, I believe, to providing empirical evidence to support constructivist theory and give both scholars and practitioners a better understanding of the international system.

Legal Rules and the Changing International System

A second reason that points to the need for interdisciplinary research is the changing nature of the international system. In chapter 5, I argued that the international system is moving in the direction of neomedievalism. If such a system were to emerge, it will become extremely difficult to determine what kind of legal rules exist and to identify when a particular rule has come into existence. With a variety of actors, there could be both "interstate law" and "international law," law common to *all* actors. If the practice of these actors remains the means of creating legal rules, strong collaboration between international legal scholars and international relations scholars will be necessary to understand this practice.

In particular, I would assert, scholars will need to work together to answer a series of questions. First, they will need to determine when a new actor has emerged. This requires the insights of international relations scholars who can assess when a particular entity is actually playing some kind of independent role in the system, and the insights of legal scholars who can determine the juridical nature of the actor. Second, these scholars will need to determine when such an actor is participating in "authoritative practice." In other words, they will be required to determine when activities of the actor are perceived to be authoritative and thus intended to give rise to the creation of legal rules. This requires both a thorough knowledge of the inner workings of the actor and its process of interaction—a knowledge to be gained from the disciplinary tools of both law and political science. Third, these investigators will also need to understand how actors are responding to each other. When a particular actor engages in authoritative practice, how do others react? Once again, this requires a thorough understanding of international interactions and a familiarity with the cues that actors give to indicate whether they perceive a certain type of behavior to be authoritative. It requires the skills of legal scholars and international relations scholars.

In short, I believe that as the international system undergoes fundamental change and moves into unfamiliar territory, the need for interdisciplinary collaboration will be even greater than it is at present. Without the different lenses of international relations and international law,[7] it will be impossible to gain an accurate understanding of an even more complex international system. Without collaborative efforts, both scholars and those diplomats who practice the art of international relations will have an imperfect picture of the world. It is my hope that this work can serve as one more useful step in the direction of promoting such collaboration.

NOTES

1. Hedley Bull, *The Anarchical Society* 13 (1977).

2. Id.

3. Id.

4. It should be noted that any number of plausible definitions of international society are conceivable. Professor Adam Watson in his classic work, *The Evolution of International Society* 4 (1992) follows Bull's definition. Professor Martin Wight offers a similar definition. Wight explains:

> *The concept of a society of states, or family of nations:* although there is no political superior, nevertheless recognition that the multiplicity of sovereign states forms a moral and cultural whole, which imposes certain moral and psychological and possibly even legal (according to some theories of law) obligations—even if not political ones. As Burke observed: "The writers on public law have often called this *aggregate* of nations a commonwealth."

Martin Wight, *International Theory: The Three Traditions* 7 (edited by Gabriele Wight & Brian Porter, 1991).

5. Or, as Bull terms it, a "great society of all mankind." Hedley Bull, *The Anarchical Society*, at 20.

6. My friend and collaborator Robert Beck has written an excellent examination of this trend toward collaboration and its prospects for the future. He has inspired much of my writing on this subject. See Robert J. Beck, International Law and International Relations: The Prospects for Interdisciplinary Collaboration, in Robert J. Beck, Anthony Clark Arend & Robert D. Vander Lugt, eds., *International Rules: Approaches from International Law and International Relations* 3 (1996).

7. A recent article employs this metaphor. Robert O. Keohane, Comment: International Relations and International Law: Two Optics, 38 *Harv. Int'l L.J.* 487 (1997).

INDEX